Fr. Slavko Barbarić,

Director:
Fr. Mario Knezović

Editor:
Krešimir Šego

Proof-reader:
Schwanhild Heintschel-Heinegg

Translator:
Isabel Bettwy

Printed Under Contract by:
The Medjugorje Web
772 N Peace Road
DeKalb, IL 60115
(815)748-0410
http://www.medjugorje.org

BARBARIĆ, Slavko

Adore My Son With Your Heart
Slavko Barbarić. - Međugorje:
Informativni centar Mir, 2003

ISBN: 978-0-9727445-1-5

Fr. Slavko Barbarić. O.F.M.

Adore My Son
With Your Heart

CONTENTS

FOREWORD

Adore My Son With Your Heart is the fifth in a series of books that Father Slavko has given us. All five are inspired by the messages of Medjugorje and thus centered around prayer. All five could come under one title of the original one, *Pray With the Heart.*

This book succeeds in answering the questions: How do we pray in front of the Most Holy Sacrament? What do we say to Jesus there? Fr. Slavko does not teach us the morals of prayer in this book; instead, he prays with us. Therefore unintentionally and in a very gentle way, he does teach and lead us into prayer. This is the fruit of numerous encounters with Him. The author simply and easily guides us into the depths of prayer, but not so deep as to cause us fear of the depths and not so far that we might find ourselves out of our depth, unable to perceive. He leads us just deep enough to feel its freshness. This book leads us along the path where, should we decide to, we can continue alone or even stop and go ahead in our own way. If, for example, the reader finds the cited Holy Scripture too long, he or she can shorten it, making a summary so as not to lack continuity, or leave it out altogether should that be desired. Here both Holy Scripture and the messages are given new life. Just like the messages given to the visionaries in Medjugorje, Fr. Slavko reflects Our Lady's simplicity and clarity in avoiding complicated ideas or difficult words.

Yet, while being simple, do not be deceived into thinking that it lacks force or theological foundation. ON the contrary, for it gently lifts us like an airplane to the heights of the 'Prayer of Adoration'. There, the author leads us into the darker corners of our souls where he knows the Lord is waiting to meet us, heal us and to liberate us.

It is most definitely a book for our times because it helps mankind to stop and to take those necessary steps into the heart. For this reason, we should be very happy to finally have it at our fingertips. With it, we really can learn to adore Jesus with our whole heart in the Most Holy Sacrament.

Sr. Marija Ancila Bubalo

INTRODUCTION

One of the most beautiful definitions of prayer is: "Prayer is life in love with God!"

We Christians have occasionally been criticized for the 'wordiness' of our prayer or for the hurried manner in which we carry it out. These criticisms may be valid, Jesus strongly criticized the practice of prayer that remains a verbal ritual and that never leads to a change in life. He also criticized prayer that seeks only to fulfill our needs, comparing it to 'pagan prayer'.

Therefore, our prayer can actually be atheistic or, in other words, without God. For example, this happens when we ask of God what we ourselves need, rather than seeking God for who He is. Jesus teaches us that God knows everything, that He loves us, that He is ready to give us everything, that the most important thing for us is to seek His righteousness and all else will then follow. This does not mean that we should not tell Jesus our needs, lay before Him our troubles or look for His help in trials. On the contrary, He Himself instructs us:

"Ask and it shall be given, seek and you shall find, knock and the door shall be opened unto you; for to whosoever asks will be given, and whosoever seeks shall find and whosoever knocks the door shall be opened unto him." (Mt 6:7-8)

Yet, if our prayer ends here, then it is a 'Godless' prayer, for it does not seek God for who He is, but for what we want from Him. God's desire is not that we should call on Him only in times of need, but that we should always be with Him.

Many Christians say that they suffer prayer 'crises'. They are convinced that they cannot pray or that they do not have time to do so. They always try to resolve problems in just about every other way and, only if nothing else works, do they then 'try God' as if He was an 'emergency help unit'! But then, as soon as the problem is solved, they put God back into His little box where they found Him and, if no other problem arises, contact with Him becomes no longer 'necessary'!

From this, we can see that the basic problem is our relationship with God or, in other words, with our faith. There are many different types of prayer.

The Church possesses a wealth of expressive prayers, texts and hymns. This is good in itself, but it no longer satisfies the soul of modern man. Our soul is exposed to a great variety of information and images every day and it longs for something that can grant it peace, stillness and quiet so that it can then meet with God. The point of all prayer and hymns is to enter into a new divine rhythm where it is possible to dwell with God in peace.

That is why the most fitting of all prayer is Adoration. We have said that prayer can be Godless when, instead of seeking God, we are always seeking things from Him. It is precisely here that Adoration is the exception. As soon as we make time for Jesus in the Most Holy Sacrament of the Altar, intending to spend that time 'with Him and for Him', we are seeking Him only because He is there! He is Emmanuel – God with us. We are not seeking Him because He can give us something, or because He is listening to us. From the time we start the prayer of Adoration, we show Him that it is Him whom we are seeking, Him whom we are adoring and praising and Him whom we are blessing and thanking.

Faith and love are the conditions of Adoration. After all, it is not easy for us to stay for a long time with someone whom we do not trust or love. This is also the case in our relationship with God because faith and love grow and develop with one another. When our love increases towards someone, the need for words to understand decreases, thereby, leaving more time for silence. The silence penetrated into the depths of our hearts and souls and, there, reaches that tranquility in God rather than in the things that He created.

The pace of this idolatrous, materialist and Godless time in which we live pushes our hearts far from the presence of God.

Thus, many Christians remain empty and alone or in frightening trials, without hope or enlightenment, or in bitter suffering, without the necessary spiritual nourishment that God gives to us all. It is in this spiritual vacuum that Adoration is urgently needed. To acknowledge God in the heart, to give Him priority, to listen to Him, to find rest in Him, to make conscious offerings to Him, to recognize and identify ourselves in Him – these are all urgent needs for today's Christians. Only through Adoration can man recognize God in His people and accept and live with them in love. Thus, a positive relationship develops with God, as Creator, and with oneself as well as with others, as the created.

Many shocking facts tell us that humanity is on the road to destruction and this happens only because it distances itself from God. In turn, this means that we distance ourselves from light and from life, from truth and from love. The human heart cannot accept this condition peacefully and here we find the reason for the existence of so much violence and destruction today.

What happens to a child if it never experiences parental love? The child searches for love in other ways without the necessary discernment as to which are the best ways. In this way, it causes destruction to itself and to those around it. This can also happen to the world. The child is searching for love but, in fact, it drives away others and finds itself in a vicious circle of its own desires, with an ever increasing desire for love that it cannot get from others because they, in turn, feel a need to defend themselves from it. And so they push the child away and do not accept it. Today's world is in danger on many levels because it lacks God and peace in Him so much that it is becoming self-destructive. Only He who created life can again restore that deep desire for life in us and He can do it only when humanity – His creation – again reveres and abandons itself to Him. Only by casting itself into the wonderful light of God's presence, can humanity be saved from its progressive deterioration and be protected from the perils of this world! Only when we do so, can we pray without ceasing, ever glorifying and adoring Him.

In Her teachings and in Her messages, the Queen of Peace strongly urges that we adore Jesus in the Most Holy Sacrament of the Altar.

"Tonight also, dear children, I am grateful to you in a special way for being here. Unceasingly adore the Most Blessed Sacrament of the Altar. I am always present when the faithful are adoring. Special graces are then being received." (March 15, 1984)

The parish community, together with the pilgrims, has responded to this message by spending some time in Adoration on Thursdays (after evening Mass), while on Wednesdays and Saturdays there is an hour of Adoration later in the evening. The Chapel of Adoration is also open throughout the day where the Blessed Sacrament is exposed.

Our Lady has asked Jelena Vasilj's prayer group to spend the entire night of the first Saturday of the month in Adoration of the Blessed Sacrament. Many other prayer groups have understood this message and have put it into practice by organizing 'holy hours', with some organizing first Saturday nights in prayer before the Blessed Sacrament right through until Sunday morning. The 'Oasis of Peace', a community founded by the Passionist priest, Gianni Sgreva, of Verona, Italy, has established perpetual Adoration in its Community in Bijakovici.

Our Lady's wish, however, is that we not only recognize Christ's presence in the Blessed Sacrament, but that we discover His constant presence and become increasingly open to Him. And it is particularly important to mention that She wishes us to recognize God in one another and that we love one another just as God loved humanity in Jesus Christ.

"Dear children! Today, more than ever, I am calling you to pray. May your life become a continuous prayer. Without love, you cannot pray. That is why I am calling you to love God, the Creator of your lives, above all else. Then you will come to know God and will love Him in everything as He loves you. ..." (November 25, 1992)

PRACTICAL INSTRUCTIONS

Dear Friend!

If you wish to use this little book during the time that you will consecrate to Jesus in the Blessed Sacrament, then read on. Because He is Emmanuel – God with us – these instructions will help us during those precious moments when we return love for His love and are present with Him in this special way.

1) If you are alone adoring Jesus, then mediate on the Scriptures in silence. Contemplate the messages that are given for every hour of Adoration and then make time for silence. A brief meditation before or after the text is only a suggestion to assist you. With it, you can more easily enter into the depths of the soul and there meet with God, hidden in the host, so that He, in turn, can enter into your soul and stay with you there.

We live in a time when our consciousness is so easily and superficially directed and re-directed that we become deaf and blind to what is really going on inside us and around us. Our heart is made for a deep experience of peace, it is created for the Word of God. In these so hurried times, we must take steps to become good and fruitful soil in which the seed of the Word of God can then grow. We must find time for repetitious prayer that consists of important words and phrases. We must never tire of repeating! It is important for our descent into the depths of the heart and soul, into the depths of the conscience and beyond the conscience – that area of our being from where the Word of God can bring forth fruit.

2) When you have made your way down that road
where you can tell Jesus everything and unburden yourself,
then you must remain in silence and in your heart
converse with Him. Take time. This is not some trick but
rather a meeting with a friend who wishes to listen to you,
who does not pass judgment when He listens to you and
who does not push you away. Learn to speak with Him!
Only in this way, can you achieve an intimate friendship.

3) It is never good to think only of oneself, so also
with prayer: include others, talk to Jesus about them too,
about all those you love as well as those who are not dear
to you, those who have caused you ill or are a source of
bitterness or pain in your heart. In this way, your love for
them will grow, reconciliation will become possible, peace
will return and it will be easier to understand them. You
will become a new person. You will change your
relationship towards others and, in this way, you will be
proof of God's love. In Adoration, you will achieve a new
communion with Jesus, you will better understand Him,
you will love Him more and He will give you the strength
for new interpersonal and Christian relationships with
others.

4) If you are at Adoration with others, then carry out
as a group what is suggested for Adoration alone. Let
someone guide the prayer who has experience with prayer.
If possible, sing together while being careful to sing songs
that the whole community knows. It is of practical help to
have a hymn rehearsal every so often before Adoration.

The most convenient hymns are short prayerful ones that can be sung repeatedly.

Do not forget that, for every meeting, we need time and space, conversation and song, quietness and silence. Just as one does not hurry when praying alone, so also one does not when praying together. Decide to devote yourself to Jesus and abandon your time to Him. Haste is always and obstacle to meaningful encounters, be they with God or with others.

5) If a priest guides Adoration or, at least, comes to it towards the end, then it is to be expected that he would give a Eucharistic blessing or a prayer for healing in body and soul. He can pray in silence while the faithful can sing quiet invocations or, after prayer, the priest can sing from time to time 'Kyrie Eleison' or something suitable as a healing prayer. The priest can then give the blessing from the altar or he can – slowing and with dignity – pass through the church, blessing the faithful with the Most Holy Sacrament, while the faithful pray in silence or sing quietly, praising and glorifying Jesus.

Both the priest and the faithful should behave in a very dignified manner. Sufficient time should be given for the soul of every 'adorer' to immerse itself in the mystery of the Eucharistic presence. It is here that we meet Jesus and it is here, if it is the Father's will (*for it is His will that is best for us*), that we are healed in body and spirit.

6) We should not forget to mention behavior during Adoration. When praying, the normal position is kneeling, but posture during prayer should not be an end in itself. For instance, when someone hurts too much while

kneeling, then kneeling is pointless. It is recommended that every person finds the position that most helps him to compose himself and be present and calm in soul and in spirit. This could be either kneeling, sitting, half kneeling or half sitting. When one enters a church where the Blessed Sacrament is already exposed, one genuflects on both knees and in silence, finds a suitable place, a comfortable position, and then remains there in silence. The outward pose is very important for assisting the interior disposition in prayer. Care must be taken that sitting or kneeling does not impede breathing and that the spine is not overburdened.

7) If the members of the prayer group are familiar with each other and not too many in number, they can occasionally (*either at the beginning or towards the end, perhaps after a longer hymn*) invite spontaneous prayers of thanksgiving, praise or blessing. Long prayers must be avoided at all costs. Short invocations are the best and should be loud and clear enough for everyone to hear and to participate in, then continuing the invocation within their own heart. The more dynamic the group, the more silence should follow the invocations. These prayers can be independent of one another or they can continue one after the other, following the train of thought of the prior invocation, grouped together like a bouquet of different flowers. Such invocations can follow one another immediately. Care must be taken that the prayer does not become repetitious, affected or forceful.

Prayer should be relaxed, devoted and with a dignity worthy of the presence of the Lord. It is also good to intersperse these prayers with appropriate songs.

8) Our invocations or outpourings of the soul should be inspired by deep faith, love, hope and a positive experience. They can also take the form of the pouring out of one's troubles, fears and trials or they can be decisions, consecrations and acts of abandonment. Adoration of this type is not suitable for groups of more than fifty members because many, who would otherwise grow from this type of prayer, will then exclude themselves from this process. Above all, we must control the theological content. Christ must be central and faith in His presence and conversion towards Him must be the group's only objective and focus. The members can use ordinary language coming from the depths of the soul or from the Word of God, in other words, from the Holy Bible.

9) It is always better to invite someone to prepare and guide the Adoration than to improvise, provided that repetition can be avoided and the richness and dynamism so vital to Adoration can be ensured. If there are any changes, it is useful to mention them at the beginning of the prayer meeting, because things that are instigated later and not explained at the start can disturb the soul and distracts our thoughts and feelings from prayer, thereby rendering the entire experience superficial. Every unplanned sound such as the moving of chairs can easily disturb the serene atmosphere that is so necessary to Adoration.

10) From time to time, it is also useful to take the opportunity outside Adoration as a prayer group to talk about your experiences and difficulties, to listen to suggestions and to try and eliminate problems. Then the

experience of one group can help another. This is a
testimony to God's love that can illuminate the way for
others and will then help us to understand ourselves and
the others. In this way, love and trust for one another is
also able to develop. When someone unburdens himself,
the members of group must look upon this as a secret
entrusted to them and keep it that way with those not in
the group.

JESUS, THE FIRST PLACE IN MY HEART BELONGS TO YOU

1) Jesus, I believe that You are present here.
  - Increase my faith!
  (*Repeat this invocation quietly within yourself*)

2) Jesus, I love You. You alone are love, real and eternal love – the Father's eternal love towards us.
  - Jesus, set my love aflame!
  (*Repeat this invocation quietly within yourself*)

3) Jesus, You are present here in the Eucharist to Become God with me and for me. You remain in this bread of the Eucharist, so that You can be my food and my life. Yours is a perceptive love, unparalleled in its simplicity. You have wrapped Yourself up in celestial silence and, in this way, You offer me only Yourself. Than You, Jesus, that You are here with me. Thank You, Jesus, that You desire that I be here with You.
  - Jesus, awaken in me the desire to be with You!
  (*Repeat this invocation quietly within yourself*)

4) Jesus, with a heart now full of desire for You, I invite You to come into my heart, into my soul, into my life, into my past and into my present! Come and take first place in my heart. From now on, it belongs only to You. Just as You give all of Yourself and open Yourself up to me wholeheartedly without ever holding anything back, in the same way, I give my heart to You just as it is now. You desire that my heart be completely clean, good, free, merciful, joyful, full of love, patience and generosity. You

wish my heart to become like Yours. Jesus, I too desire this:

- Come, Jesus, and make my heart like Yours!
  (*Repeat this invocation quietly within yourself*)

5) My Jesus, as I am praying that You make my heart like Yours and that You take first place in my life. I beg You to illuminate me with Your Holy Spirit, so that I can recognize all within me that is not the Father's will and which keeps me from You. I present to You my past and my present, all that I feel and experience, anything that allows negative traces and effects to remain within me. I present to You all my problems and illnesses, everything in me that resists God's will. I offer You anything that creates insubordination or disobedience to God's Word, anything that hinders the realizing of that Word.

- Jesus receive my prayer!
  (*Repeat this invocation quietly within yourself*)

6) Thank You, Jesus, that You have listened to me. I know that You know everything about me, but it helps me to tell You everything. Jesus, speak now to my heart! I wish to listen to You. Let my heart be ready, let it rejoice in Your Word, let it understand.

"...no one can be the slave of two masters. He will either hate the first and love the second or be attached to the first and despise to second. You cannot be the slave of both God and money. That is why I am telling you not to worry about your life and what you are to eat and what you are to wear. Surely life is more than food and the body more than clothing! So do not worry, do not say: 'What are we to eat? What are we to drink? What are we to wear?' Your

heavenly Father knows you need them all. Set your hearts on His kingdom first and on His saving justice, and all these other things will be given you as well." (Mt 6:24-25, 31-33)
(Remain in silence and let the Word of Life echo within you)

7) Jesus, thank You for Your Word! May it resonate within me and chase away my doubts, all my lack of faith, all my anxieties and worries, and may I, above all, be enthusiastic about searching for Your reign. May I always believe that I can abandon everything to my Father who loves me. Liberate me from all that is weighing me down and make me completely Yours! I believe that You can do this. Our times are immersed in atheism that has its own worries, weights and fears. Jesus, thank You for having sent Mary, our Mother, teacher and Queen of Peace. Already when She first appeared, She said:
"Dear children, I have come to tell you that God exists!"

Thank You, Jesus, for allowing Her to come and invite me so often that I open myself, that I abandon myself, that I give You the first place in my life! She advised me to meditate upon Your word that I have just heard once a week.

- Jesus, I give You my whole self – body, spirit and soul!

(Repeat this prayer quietly within yourself)

8) Jesus, I adore You now with Mary. I wish to listen to Your word and to follow it with Her. In Her life, You always had the first place. She gave You Her heart when She said: "Here I am Lord, be it done unto me according to Your will."

- Lord, let it also be done unto me according to Your will!

(Repeat this invocation quietly within yourself)

9) Jesus, You came for the good of all and, for this reason, I wish to pray, not only for myself, but for my family, my parents, brothers, sisters, friends, community and for the whole world.

(Remain in silence, and speak to Jesus of those who are foremost in your heart)

Many in the world call themselves Christians, but You are distant from them because their hearts and souls are occupied by the things of the world. I wish to pray for all Christians.

(Remain in silence ...)

Many do not know You, even though You came for everyone. The hearts of many are empty. They follow false gods, destroying the lives of others as well as their own. I want to pray now, together with Mary and with all who believe in You, for the grace of faith for them.

(Remain in silence...)

Many have given themselves over to evil and follow its paths, doing evil to themselves and to others. Be merciful to them, Jesus, and give them back the freedom which You impart when You are in the heart of man.

(Remain in silence...)

Send Your Spirit and illuminate the hearts that are clouded by the darkness of doubt and the slavery of sin so that they may enter into the freedom of the children of God!

(Remain in silence...)

10) Blessing

(If a priest leads Adoration, he can raise the Blessed Sacrament and pray a blessing. If praying alone, then, with faith, ask for blessing and healing.)

Jesus, heal my faith and trust in You, prevent all mistrust, fear and anxiety. Heal my conscience and my subconscious so that I may increasingly live in Your presence! Heal my love and my hope! Jesus, I beg You with the faith of Your Church, heal the sick and disabled! May all now begin to hope in Your blessing.

Drive Satan far from us and restrain him in his actions. Bless me, my family, my people and the whole world with peace! Send Your Spirit and renew the face of the earth. Bless and defend us, You who live and reign world without end! Amen.

JESUS, I YEARN FOR YOUR FACE

1) I adore You, Jesus! You are my God. Thank You for having an ardent desire to be among mankind! This means You have an ardent desire to also be with me.

May You be blessed for the love that inspired You to remain with me in this way! Your yearning to be with me is put into effect so simply. You are present in this Host. Almighty God, Son of God, hidden in this little Host. Infinite mystery! I believe and I adore You!

- I yearn for Your face, Jesus!
  (Repeat this prayer quietly within yourself)

2) The Psalmist sings:

"Yahweh is my light and my salvation, whom should I fear?
Yahweh is the fortress of my life, whom should I dread? When the
wicked advance on me to eat me up, they, my opponents, my enemies
are the ones who fall.
Though an army pitch tent against me; my heart will not fear, though
war break out against me, my trust will never be shaken.
One thing I ask of Yahweh, one thing I seek: to dwell in Yahweh's
house all the days of my life, to enjoy the sweetness of Yahweh, to
seek out his temple.
For he hides me away under his roof on the day of evil, he folds me in
the recesses of his tent, sets me high on a rock.
Now my head is held high above the enemies who surround me; in
his tent, I will offer sacrifices of acclaim.
I will sing, I will make music for Yahweh.
Yahweh, hear my voice as I cry, pity me, answer me!
Of you my heart has said : "Seek His face."
Your face, Yahweh, I seek; do not turn away from me.

*Do not thrust aside Your servant in anger, without You, I am
helpless.
Never leave me, never forsake me God, my Savior.
Though my father and my mother forsake me, Yahweh will gather
me up.* (Ps 27: 1-10)

> - Your face, Lord, I seek. I yearn for Your face!
>   (*Repeat this prayer quietly within yourself*)

3) Jesus, may You be thanked, blessed and praised
forever. May the heavens and the earth, the angels and all
the saints exalt You and the whole Church sing Your
praises because You did not consider it below You to stay
with me in such a simple way! Your presence is a deep
reality for me, it is the truth of Your Church and all the
faithful.

May Your deep desire to live with me awaken a
profound yearning and desire within me to be with You!
May my heart, like that of the Psalmist, continually say
"Seek the face of the Lord!" Give me the grace that I may
love and yearn for You in the same way as You love and
yearn for me!

> - Grant that I may love You the way You love
>   me!
>   (*Repeat this prayer quietly within yourself*)

4) The Psalmist inspires me with a continual sigh
for You, O Lord. I listen to his words and follow them
with my heart. May this next psalm be a song, a sigh, an
exultation of my soul!

"As a deer yearns for running streams, so I yearn for You, my God.

I thirst for God, the living God; when shall I go to see the face of God?
I have no food but tears day and night, as all day long I am taunted: Where is your God?
This I remember as I pour out my heart, how I used to pass under the roof of the Most High, used to go to the house of God, among cries of joy and praise, the sound of the feast:
Why be so downcast, why all these sighs?
Hope in God! I will praise him still, my Savior, my God.
When I am downcast, I think of You: from the land of Jordan and Hermon, I think of You, humble mountain.
Deep is calling to deep by the roar of Your cataracts, all Your waves and breakers have rolled over me.
In the daytime God sends His faithful love, and even at night; the song it inspired in me is a prayer to my living God.
I shall say to God, my rock: "Why have You forgotten me? Why must I go around in mourning harassed by the enemy?" With death in my bones my enemies taunt me, all day long they ask me, Where is your God?
Why so downcast, why all these sighs, o my soul.
Hope is God!
I will praise Him still, my Savior, my God." (Ps 42: 1-12)

- May my soul yearn for You, as a deer yearns for running streams.

(Repeat this prayer quietly within yourself)

5) Jesus, You are enflamed with love and yearning for us. You wish to be our love, our peace, our life, our truth, our way, our fount of living waters. You wish to serve all, with Your love so that we may live happily, loving one another.

I recognize, Jesus, that my desires and my longings are often distant from You. This world often distracts me and takes the first place in my thoughts and desires, my feelings and endeavors. I am so far away from the You. People and things take precedence and worldly desires and enjoyments take my attention from You. Too easily I trust that the world and all its belongings can bring me happiness and peace, that it can uplift my soul: These are yearnings that draw me towards the world.

Kneeling before You, I beg You that, during this time spent in Adoration, You cleanse my heart and soul, You heal my memories and feelings and draw to Yourself all my longings and strivings so that You become everything to me.

Grant, Jesus, that my heart finds peace in You, and that all my yearnings find their answer in You. Grant, Jesus, that You become my first and my last, my complete yearning and desire, that You take first place in my words, thoughts, feelings and deeds.

- Jesus, liberate me and direct my heart and mind to You!)
  (Repeat this invocation quietly within yourself)

6) Jesus, I adore You and I thank You that you wish to be the light, the peace, the love, the yearning, the way and the life of our families, of fathers and mothers, of parents and children, of the young and the old, the sick and the healthy! You wish to be 'God with them' and in them. May You be blessed, praised and exalted in our families! May You become the yearning of our families that, in this way, they may open themselves up to peace and joy, love and togetherness. You know that in many

families You have been forgotten, Jesus. Fathers and mothers have forgotten You and children have not come to know You. You remain a stranger to many families. Many have been distracted by the world, by enjoyment and by wealth. Atheism and divorce have gained so much ground, opening the road to destruction. Forgive our families, liberate them and be Emmanuel – God with our families – today.

Awaken in us the yearning for Your face! May our families be free from all deception, from all sinful yearnings and all misguidance. Develop within us a deep awareness of Your presence in families and grant that they convert, find peace, strengthen themselves and find happiness, living God- filled lives.

(Remain in silence and think specifically about your family or about those with whom you live)

7) Jesus, I adore You, because, I too, am part of Your Church, a member of Your mystical body. I adore You, together with the whole Church of which You are the head, Mary is the Mother and the Holy Spirit its Defender and Advocate. You gave the Church to the world so that it may continue Your works, bear witness to your love and show Your presence in the world.

May the yearning for Your face continually blaze like the burning bush within Your Church, within every heart that is marked by Baptism and by Confirmation, cleansed by the grace of forgiveness and nourished by Your Eucharistic Body. May a new flame of yearning for Your face be enkindled in every heart that is turned more towards the created than the Creator. May a flame of yearning for Your face set alight everything within our hearts and souls so that Your Church, with all its members, may shine with a new testifying radiance for You.

(Pray in silence for priests, confessors, bishops, the Pope)

8) Jesus, I adore You, together with the whole world that is created by You, together with all its peoples and races who do not yet know You, but have sought You sincerely in nature and in the stars, those who pursue the deep longing in their hearts and continually search but still have not discovered You. Grant that they may meet those who, with their lives and with their sharing will cause them to discover You as the answer to all their yearning and desires! May they find You! May their hearts be calmed, and may they find joy and a new beginning in You!

I present to You also those who knew You, but have consciously rejected You, led astray by sin. I pray to You now for all those in darkness, because Your Mother has invited me to do so.

"Dear children! In your life, you have all experienced light and darkness. God lets every person recognize good and evil. I am calling you to the light, which you should carry to all the people who are in darkness. Daily people who are in darkness come into your homes. Dear children, give them the light! Thank you for having responded to my call." (March 14, 1985)

\-   Jesus, have mercy on all mankind through the Intercession of Mary, the Queen of Peace!

(Repeat this prayer quietly within yourself)

9) Jesus, I present to You those who have poisoned their hearts and souls, pulled by a desire for alcohol, drugs and bodily pleasures. They are tired because their hearts have become empty and they have lost all respect for themselves and for others; they kill themselves quietly and slowly, wandering the ways of this world, but they are really longing for salvation. Jesus, be their salvation, their love and desire. Pull them up from where they have fallen; return them to the good road, and open to them a fount of new life!

(Present to Jesus all those who you know have similar problems)

10) Blessing

Jesus, You are the yearning and love of all the saints and all the upright, the desire and love of our Mother Mary. Bless us here now, our families, our prayer groups, all communities in the Church and the Church itself! Say the word and awaken a burning desire for You within me.

Open my eyes just as You opened the eyes of the blind that I may see and love You, and that I burn for You. Heal those who have weakened their souls through evil habits and, in this way, have fallen into illness and other problems! Enlighten this world so that every heart finds itself yearning and loving You – You the only and true God in the Holy Spirit who lives and reigns world without end. Amen.

SPEAK, LORD,
YOUR SERVANT IS LISTENING

1) I adore You, Jesus! I believe in You with living faith, and I love You with an ardent love. You are present here and even though You have wrapped Yourself up in Godly silence, I know that You wish to communicate with me. Speak to me in a way that my heart hears and understands! I wish to meet You now as my Lord, who unceasingly invites and expects me. I am coming now exactly as I am. I wish to adore You, to believe in You and love You because you are God, our credible witness, worthy of every praise and love.

- I adore You, I believe in You and I love You, Jesus, Word of the Father!

(Repeat this prayer quietly within yourself)

2) Jesus, You are the eternal Word of the Father. Through You, all things were made. You have the Word of eternal life. Your Word is almighty. I bless You and glorify You, I adore You and thank You because the Father speaks to me through You. I now wish to listen and to hear You.

- Speak to my heart, Jesus, I wish to listen to You!

(Repeat this prayer quietly within yourself)

3) May Your Spirit who spoke to the Father and the prophets be active in me now. May He act in me now as He acted since the beginning of the world. I know that I sometimes listened, but did not understand. My heart then was like the rocky ground upon which the seed fell.

Your words started to bring forth fruit from my heart, but the worries and troubles of this world destroyed them. Forgive me Lord!

Jesus, now I really want to listen to Your Word, and I want it to bring forth abundant fruit. Send me Your Holy Spirit! Let Him cleanse the soil of my heart, clear away every rock, every thorn and every bad root that chokes the growth and development of Your Word!

- Lord, purify my heart that it may readily accept Your Word!

(Repeat this invocation quietly within yourself)

4) I wish to hear and be obedient to Your Word, just as Mary, Your Mother, did. O, how intent upon the Words of the Holy Scriptures She was when, as a child and young girl, She listened to them! How She absorbed the words, how She derived pleasure from them and how much light, direction and response to the questions and longings of Her heart She found! I wish to listen in the same way She listened in that moment when the angel announced that She was to become Your Mother. With how much humility and openness She replied: "Let it be done unto me according to Your word!"

Mary, I want to thank You that You are together with me at Adoration, that You wish to pray with me, that You help me listen to the Word of Your Son and teach me to take care of it in my heart like a precious pearl! O Mary, keep vigil over the Word of Your Son in my heart!

- Mary, teach me to listen to and invoke the Word of Jesus!

(Repeat this prayer quietly within yourself)

O Mary, You wish me to love the Word of God the way You loved it and, for this reason, You say in the message: ***"Dear children! Today, I call on you to read the Bible every day in your homes and let it be in a visible place so as always to encourage you to read it and to pray. Thank you for having responded to my call."*** (October 18, 1984)

- Mary, I now decide to do what You say.

(In silence, decide what you will do, in what visible place you will put the Bible in your home, or decide perhaps to keep a copy of the New Testament always with you)

5) Lord, Jesus, I beg You now to speak to parents and the elderly in families so that they may all respect and love Your Word. May they watch over it in their hearts and help their children to listen and obey it. May what happened in the family of Eli and Samuel also take place in our own families. This is written for us in the first book of Samuel:

"Now the boy Samuel was serving Yahweh in the presence of Eli; in those days it was rare for Yahweh to speak; visions were uncommon. One day it happened that Eli was lying down in his room. His eyes were beginning to grow dim; he could no longer see. The lamp of God had not yet gone out, and Samuel was lying in Yahweh's sanctuary; where the ark of God was, when Yahweh called: "Samuel! Samuel!" He answered: "Here I am!" and, running to Eli, he said: "Here I am as you called me!" Eli said: "I did not call. Go back and lie down." So he went and lay down. And again Yahweh called: "Samuel! Samuel!" He got up and went to Eli and said: "Here I am as you called me!" He replied: "I did not call, my son; go back and lie down." As yet, Samuel had no knowledge of Yahweh and the word of Yahweh had not been

revealed to him. Again Yahweh, was called the third time. He got up and went to Eli and said: "Here I am as you called me." Eli then understood that Yahweh was calling the child, and he said to Samuel: "Go and lie down, and if someone calls, say: Speak, Yahweh; for your servant is listening." So Samuel went and lay down in his place. Yahweh then came and stood by, calling as He had done before, "Samuel! Samuel!" and Samuel answered, "Speak Yahweh, as Your servant is listening." (1 Sam 3: 1-10)

- Speak, Jesus, and may our families be open to Your Word!
(Repeat this invocation quietly within yourself)

6) Jesus, You entrusted Your Word to the Apostles and, through them, Your Church that they bring the Good News to the ends of the earth. While I adore You now and wish to hear Your Words, I bring before You the Pope, all bishops, priests, catechists, especially my parish priest, and all those who help him. Send them Your Holy Spirit so that they are always ready to give priority to Your Word. Grant that their hearts become instructed by Your Word. Remove all that obstructs them from listening to and understanding Your Word, so that they, in the power of Holy Spirit, can bring the Good News to the world as You wished.
(In silence, bring before Jesus your parish priest, his helpers and catechists)

7) Jesus, You wish that Your Word reaches the ends of the earth, all people and nations, because Your Word is truth and light. Many people live in darkness because they have not yet heard Your Word. It has not yet reached

them and they follow false gods and listen to them. O Jesus, call many young people today to bring Your Word to pagan peoples and grant Your grace to all nations that they may readily hear and accept Your Word! May the strength of Your Spirit follow the missionaries so that their words may be accompanied by signs that will cause hearts to open to You!

(Pray in silence for missionaries and pagan people)

8) Jesus, in today's world there are so many voices – radio, television, newspapers, films and many other means are at mankind's disposal. Jesus, I would like to put before You all those who have control over the media, newspapers, publicity agencies, television stations and all other means of communication. Be blessed for all those who use technical means to proclaim the truth. Grant that they effectively invite to love and forgiveness, and that they lead those who listen to them to good and noble ends. Follow their works and make them bring forth fruits in the hearts of mankind!

I pray now also for those who misuse the means of communication to spread lies, to inspire violence, to encourage sexual immorality and aid the breakdown of Christian ethics. May they convert and experience Your Word of truth and peace, and then wish to put themselves into Your service!

(In silence, examine your conscience and see if decisions ought to be made for your own life and for your family regarding your example, your outlook and your work)

9) Jesus, it is the young people in particular who are endangered by words, by such a flood of words, by so much information and so many images. But especially the young people are looking for truth, for love and peace. Speak to them, enlighten and help their parents and catechists to proclaim Your Word, so that they become inspired by Your Word that it may grow within them and bring forth abundant fruit!

(In silence, pray for the young people in your family, in your community, in your parish and, in a special way, for those who have wandered far from the path of the Word of God. Mention them by name)

10) Blessing

Jesus, Lord most holy, say Your Word to me now and heal my soul, so that it can accept it. Purify my family and every heart and enable them to listen to and fulfill Your Word. Liberate me and protect me from the spirit of lies. Drive Satan, the father of lies, far from me and far from the world. Grant me the grace to be always open to Your Word, especially when it is difficult for me! Bless all those who now await the true word from parents, friends, and those who have the task of educating them! Pronounce Your Divine Word so that their bodies and souls may be healed. Be glorified within me and make me into a witness of Your Word, You who live and reign world without end. Amen.

COME, LORD JESUS

1) I adore You, Jesus, I believe in You and I love You.
   (Repeat this prayer quietly within yourself)

2) You are present here. I believe this with all my heart and all my soul. Still I call to You: Come, Lord Jesus! Maranatha! Come, I await You with love! Come, my heart welcomes You and rejoices in Your coming. Come, I wish my soul and my whole being to soar up to You. I wish with my whole life to be one call, one yearning.

   Just as a child yearns for his mother, may my soul and body yearn and cry out for You:
   - Come Lord Jesus, Maranatha!
     (Repeat this invocation quietly within yourself)

3) Come, Lord Jesus! My heart, now united with Mary, Your Mother, invites You. Together with Her, I wish to yearn now in the same way that Her heart yearned for the Messiah, the Savior of Her people, even though She did not know that She was to be His mother. I wish to experience, together with Her, that same love and longing for You that feels like a burning within, just as Her heart burned from the moment of Your conception in Her womb up until Your death and glorious resurrection in Heaven. She invites me and instructs me:

"Dear children! Today, I invite you to give me your heart, so I can change it and make it similar to mine. You are wondering, dear children, why you cannot respond to that which I am asking from you.

You do not achieve this because you have not given me your heart, so I can change it. You talk but you do not act. I call on you to do everything that I am telling you. That way, I will be with you. Thank you for having responded to my call." (May 15, 1986)

Mary, thank You for calling me. I want to give You my heart now that it may become similar to Yours, filled with the love for Jesus. Also my heart and my soul want to say without ceasing:

- Come, Lord Jesus!
  (Repeat this invocation quietly within yourself)

4) Thank You for the word that St. John wrote in the book of Revelation:

"Do not be afraid; it is I, the first and the last; the Living One, I was dead and look I am alive for ever and ever, and I hold the keys of death and of Hades… The Spirit and the Bride say: 'Come!' Let everyone who listens answer, 'Come!' Then let all who are thirsty come: all who want it may have the water of life, and have it free. The one who attests these things says: I am indeed coming soon. Amen. 'Come Lord Jesus!'"
(Rev 1:17b-18, 22:17 and 20)

- Amen. Come Lord Jesus!
  (Repeat this invocation quietly within yourself)

5) Lord Jesus, You have said: "I am the light of the world, who follows me does not walk in darkness!" I welcome You because I believe that You are light, like the early rising sun, born to illuminate hearts and souls. I come before You and I open my heart and soul to You, so that You may enter into my heart as light, to dispel all darkness, to light up every corner of my soul, especially

those corners where wounds have crept in, and where sin and bad habits have taken root, where darkness has made its home. From the depths of my being, I cry out to You:

- Light of lights, Jesus, bathe my heart in Your light!

(Repeat this invocation quietly within yourself)

6) Lord Jesus, come into our families! They need Your light; parents need Your light that they may educate their children; sisters and brothers need Your light that they may live every moment together in faith and love; little children and young people need Your light that they may increasingly open themselves to You. Fill the hearts of parents with a yearning for You so that it may spill over into the hearts of their children!

You know, Jesus, how many families live in darkness. In many families reign disorder and anxiety which result in conflicts. Love and reconciliation have died within them. In the darkness of evil, many unborn lives have been taken, while those allowed to live suffer from the lack of light which only love can give.

(In silence, think about your own family, about families you know and intercede for all families)

7) Lord Jesus, You sent Your Church that it would be a light to the world, the city built on the hill-top, the lamp on the lampstand that shines for everyone to see.

Thank You, Jesus, for Your light that comes through the Church! May Your Church remain faithful and watchful, as Your faithful bride-to-be, awaiting You in song and prayer, in love and peace! May the Pope, the bishops and priests, communities and orders within Your

Church, await You like the wise virgin until You, the spouse, come and knock. Grant that, in all corners of the earth, Your Church continually sings songs of Your coming and in the strength of Your Spirit speaks out:

-    Come, Lord Jesus, in Your Church and through Your Church into the world!

(Repeat this invocation quietly within yourself)

8) Lord Jesus, You are the light to illuminate all peoples.   You bathe in light all those who sit in the shadow of death and darkness. I adore You and I ask You: Come, Lord Jesus, into this world and dispel its darkness! Shine there where there are wars, where there is injustice and hatred, where there is a spirit of violence and deception.

I acknowledge that my lack of light contributes to the darkness of this world. That is why now, in front of You, I renounce all that is darkness within me, my sins and all that hinders Your coming to me. Jesus, I want to pray now in the name of all who do not, cannot or who refuse to renounce darkness, so that all hearts will be open to Your coming, to Your light.

-    Jesus, light of the world, illuminate all peoples and nations!

(Repeat this invocation quietly within yourself)

9) My Jesus, thank You for letting me invite You to come in this prayer of Adoration! Thank You because You hear my voice and You prepare my heart! May I bless and thank You within my life. May Your coming completely possess me so that I become full of Your light! Make me into a witness of Yours. Through me, enter into

my family, my community, the Church and the world! Make me into that city on the hilltop, that light which You speak about. Come and shine within me, so that others may see and find You!

(In silence, present to Jesus those for whom you especially wish to pray with prayers of blessing and healing.)

10) Blessing

Lord Jesus, I believe in Your love for the sick and the disabled, for those who are in sin, those who are far from You and those who do not know You. I believe also in Your love towards those who have let their bad habits distance themselves from You and who do not pray that You come. I believe in Your love also for those who have fallen under the influence of Satan, who have consciously offered up their lives in the service of evil. Even if they work against You and try to disclaim You, You still love them.

Extend Your hands over us now and heal us! Illuminate us and send upon us the gifts of Your Holy Spirit! Touch every sick and dark corner of our hearts and souls and lead us towards You! Come there where hearts are disillusioned, where they have been left alone, divorced from You and from others! Bless us, You who live and reign world without end! Amen.

JESUS, KING OF PEACE, I ADORE YOU

1) Jesus, King of Peace, I adore You!
    Jesus, creator of eternal peace, I love You because
    You are our peace!

2) O Jesus, the hearts of mankind have yearned for
You as the King of peace for centuries. The prophets
sang of You. All peoples, all nations of all times yearned
for You as the One who brings peace. Those who were
oppressed by evil, by sin and injustice and who were led
into conflict and war have yearned for You. All those who
were endangered awaited the day when peace would dawn.
        The Psalmist in Sacred Scripture prays and sings
about peace:
*"Yahweh, you are gracious to your land, you bring back the captives
of Jacob, you take away the guilt of your people, you blot out all their
sin, you retract all your anger, you renounce the heat of your fury.*
Bring us back, God our Savior, appease your indignation against us!
Will you be angry with us forever?
Will you prolong your wrath age after age?
Will you not give us life again for your people to rejoice in you?
Show us, Lord, your faithful love, grant us your saving help.
I am listening. What is God's message?
*Yahweh's message is peace for his people, for his faithful, if only they
renounce their folly.*
*His saving help is near for those who fear him, his glory will dwell in
our land.*
*Faithful love and loyalty join together, saving justice and peace
embrace.*
*Loyalty will spring up from the earth, and justice will lean down
from Heaven.*

Yahweh will himself give prosperity, and our soil will yield its harvest.
Justice will walk before him, treading out a path."
(Ps 85: 1-14)

> \- Jesus, King of Peace, in You, meet love and faith, justice and peace!
> (Repeat this prayer quietly within yourself)

3) Jesus, King of Peace, I adore You and I praise the very moment of Your birth in Bethlehem because, that holy night, the angels announced Your plan of peace "Glory to God in the highest and peace to men of goodwill!" To glorify Your heavenly Father and to enable all peoples, brothers and sisters, to be men of goodwill – that is Your plan. Cleanse my heart now with Your Holy Spirit that I become a person of goodwill so that, from this moment on, my heart continually glorifies and thanks You and, in that way, finds true peace! Purify me from every evil inclination, from everything in me that is not yet ready to sing Your praise and which hinders me from becoming a person of goodwill! Grant, Jesus, that I become increasingly like You through Adoration. May my heart unite with the song of the angels.

> \- Glory to God in the highest and peace on earth to men of goodwill!
> *(Repeat this prayer quietly within yourself)*

4) Jesus, King of Peace, I bless and thank You, because You sent us Your Mother, the Queen of Peace.

Thank You, Mary, that You are here with us! With Your whole being, You participated in the plan of Your

Son. When You announced to the angel: "Let it be done unto me according to Your word!" You consciously committed Yourself to the plan of peace, You gave Your heart to the King of Peace. How the angels' song reverberated in Your heart while You held Your Son in Your arms! Thank You because You are here with me now. Thank You because You invite and teach me to become a person of goodwill and that I give glory to God:

"Dear children! Today, I invite you to peace. I have come here as Queen of Peace and I desire to enrich you with my motherly peace. Dear children, I love you and I desire to bring all of you to the peace, which only God gives and which enriches every heart. I invite you to become carriers and witnesses of my peace to this world without peace. May peace reign in the whole world, which is without peace and longs for peace. I bless you with my motherly blessing. Thank you for having responded to my call."
(July 25, 1990)

- Jesus, King of Peace, together with the Queen of Peace, I adore You!
    (Repeat this prayer quietly within yourself)

5) Jesus, King of Peace, I adore and thank You because You have become the King of Peace for all time. You differ from all the high powers and rulers of this world. They said of You, "It is better that one man die for the people, than that the whole people go to ruin." You even wished to give Your life, to sacrifice Yourself for me and for all people so that we do not go to our ruin. The powerful of this world want that others give up their lives for their ideas and interests, so that they can push

44

themselves to greater wealth and power. They look after their own ends at the cost of the lives of other people. Thank You, Jesus, that You show us another road! According to worldly thinking, You lost, but – in reality – You won. You are the everlasting King.

> \- Jesus, King of Peace, teach the powerful of this world Your way of Peace!
> (*Repeat this invocation quietly within yourself*)

6) Jesus, King of Peace, thank You because You gave Your Church to this world so that it would continue Your plan of peace and teach mankind to become people of goodwill. Be blessed for all that Your Church has done and continues to do for peace and for the announcement of Your peaceful kingdom! Jesus, You know that there is much disorder and conflict among those who call themselves Yours. You know every agitation and clash within the Catholic Church and every lack of understanding with other churches and communities. You said to Your Apostles that they should not be like the powerful of this world who compete for power but that they should serve one another in love. And still, many who are called to follow and serve forget Your path to peace. I am sorry, Jesus, that so many conflicts within the Church overshadow Your mission of peace. But I know also that it is in Your power to turn all to good and, therefore, I ask You:

> \- Purify Your Church and turn it into an instrument of peace!
> (*Repeat this invocation quietly within yourself*)

7) Jesus, King of Peace, it is Your wish that all our families live in peace – husbands and wives, children and parents, the old and the young. Peace will come when we are ready to accept the condition for peace and to sacrifice ourselves in love for one another. Be praised and thanked for all those families who live in peace, because they are able to love one another. Bless them and grant that they never tire! Be blessed, because You will teach the road of peace to those who are now experiencing disorder, because disorder paves the road to divorce and violent behavior which hinders the development of children, disturbs young adults and suffocates spiritual values. Thank You because Your love will lead them along the path of peace and because, by Your strength, justice and peace will meet and embrace!

(In silence, present your family, your community, and especially those who live without peace)

8) Jesus, King of Peace, I thank and bless You for those moments on the cross, when You faced Your death alone and You pronounced those words of peace, praying for those who had done You wrong! Thank You for the peace that You maintained in Your heart despite the suffering and pain! Thank You for the love with which You blessed and prayed for Your enemies, thus showing us the path of peace – forgiveness and reconciliation, prayer and thanksgiving.

Jesus, You know that our hearts are always longing for peace, that they cannot be happy if they are in conflict, if they are not reconciled with You and with those around us.

Jesus, as I thank You for the love with which You forgave. I open up my heart in the name of those who are misled and have no love within them, and who are ruled by a refusal to reconciliation.

- Jesus, King of Peace, give us the strength to reconcile and forgive!

(Repeat this invocation and present those who are involved in conflicts and those who do not seem to have the strength to forgive.)

9) Jesus, King of Peace, You said that the world cannot give peace and that true peace comes through You. Today, especially young people are in danger. Everyone is looking for peace, but many never find it because they become the pawns of false prophets who promise peace, but do not speak of forgiveness, reconciliation, justice or love. Many have fallen under the influence of drugs and alcohol, copying immoral behavior, obeying the rules of this world which cannot lead to peace. Jesus, reveal Yourself to them and be their peace. Enable every young person to say together with St. Augustine, "My heart is restless, God, until it rests in You."

- Jesus, King of Peace, be the peace of all young people!

(Repeat this prayer quietly and present to the Lord the names of young people who you know are having problems)

10) Blessing

Jesus, King of Peace, bless those here present with the depths of Your peace. Grant that Your peace touches every heart that needs it like a morning dew. May it touch every heart which is experiencing tension and strain, and every heart which is full of bitterness and pain. May Your peace overcome every conflict in our families, communities, the Church and in the world! Through the strength of Your grace, may those who have lost their peace due to suffering find peace again! May those who find reconciliation and forgiveness difficult receive the grace of peace, so that togetherness becomes possible! Be glorified, King of Peace, in all those who are sick in body and soul! Bless us all through the intercession of the Queen of Peace, You who live and reign world without end. Amen.

THIS IS MY BODY

1) I adore You, because You are present here in this host.
   I love You because it was love that inspired You to remain here with us.
   I believe in You, Jesus, because Your Word is all powerful.

2) I wish to be with You, Jesus. I want to live through the moments of the first Eucharist with You. I want to rest my head upon Your chest like St. John, Your disciple, and listen to the beat of Your heart, a heart that burned with so much love when the moment came to give Yourself up for us. St. Luke writes for us:

"When the time came, He took His place at the table, and the Apostles with Him. And He said to them: "I have ardently longed to eat this Passover with you before I suffer; because I tell you, I shall not eat it until it is fulfilled in the kingdom of God." Then, taking a cup, He gave thanks and said, "Take this and share it among you, because from now on, I tell you, I shall never again drink wine until the kingdom of God comes." Then He took the bread, and when He had given thanks, He broke it and gave it to them, saying: "This is my body given for you; do this in remembrance of me." He did the same with the cup after supper, and said: "This cup is the new covenant in my blood poured out for you."
(Lk 22:14-20)

- Jesus, You said, "This is my body, this is my blood!"
  (Repeat this prayer quietly within yourself)

3) Jesus, ever-present Lord and God, with how much love Your heart burned when You said, "I have ardently longed to eat this with you!" Son of God, Eternal Word, Holy of Holies, Infinite Love, You burn with a living desire for me. O, how great is the mystery of Your love. I am aware that I am neither worthy of Your love nor of the yearning of Your heart. I know that this does not affect You because Your love is unconditional. Jesus, omnipresent Lord, with the strength of Your Spirit, inflame now within me a deep yearning so that I yearn for You with the same love that You yearned for me. My heart is cold and without love, my heart is not capable of returning such love, but Your Spirit can empower me.

- Jesus, inflame my heart with love for You!

(Repeat this invocation quietly within yourself)

4) Jesus, the only heart which burned with the same yearning for You was that of Your Mother, Mary. In Her heart, there was the right response to Your love. She was the only one who really understood what was happening in Your heart. Together with Her, I adore You now. She is the only one who can say in front of every host: This is flesh of my flesh. For this reason, She can understand You with Her whole being as mother.

O Mary, I thank You that You are here with me at this moment when I am thanking and glorifying Your Son and our Savior, because He has remained with me in this piece of bread. Grant that by Your intercession my whole being will burn with the same love as Your motherly heart felt.

"Dear children! Today, I invite you to accept with seriousness the messages I am giving you and to live them. I am with you, dear children, and I desire that each one of you be ever closer to my heart. Therefore, little children, pray and seek the will of God in your daily life. I desire that each one of you discover the way of holiness and grow in it until eternity. I will pray for you and intercede for you before God that you comprehend the greatness of this gift, which God is giving me that I can be with you. Thank you for having responded to my call."
(April 25, 1990)

- Mary, may my heart be united with Your heart and, in that way, unite with the heart of my Lord.
(Repeat this prayer quietly within yourself)

5) Jesus, I praise and bless You for that moment when, in front of Your Apostles, You took the bread and wine and with love said the words, "Take this and eat it, take this and drink it." Be blessed for that moment when You said, "Do this in memory of me." You entrusted this to the disciples so that they could do the same at all times. Be blessed also for that moment when the Apostles started to evangelize and lay their hands on others so that Your priests could do the same. For this, I adore You, Jesus, and I bless You for every one of Your ministers who continue to do the same.

Be blessed, Jesus, in the person and in the ministry of the Holy Father, be blessed in our bishops, in all priests and in those who are preparing to work in Your Eucharistic ministry. Grant that their hearts also are filled with Your love. May they burn with the same love as You burned when You pronounced those Eucharistic words. Fill all with Your Holy Spirit, that they may worthily partake in Your priestly mission.

- Jesus, make the hearts of Your priests like Your own.
(*Repeat this invocation quietly within yourself*)

6) Be blessed, Jesus, for the moment in which, for the first time, You offered Yourself to Your disciples, and entered their lives in such a mysterious but real way. Be blessed also in the name of those who receive You in the heavenly bread and the cup of salvation at the hands of Your priests. Be blessed, Jesus, for those who daily nourish themselves spiritually with You and who believe in Your real presence in the Eucharistic bread and wine. Be blessed in all Your ministers who offer Your body saying, "The body of Christ," and in those who reply, "Amen." Jesus, grant that, by the strength of Your spirit, Eucharistic communion with You is always a meeting of love for every believer who receives You.

I am sorry for every holy communion which I made superficially, unworthy of You and Your love. That is why, today, I wish to show You more love and burn with an even deeper longing for You.

- Amen, I praise, bless and rejoice in You, Jesus.
(*Repeat this prayer quietly within yourself*)

7) I adore You, together with all those who adore You with living faith. I glorify You, together with those communities who adore You night and day. Bless them, Lord Jesus, and fill them with the Spirit of Adoration that their dwelling with You becomes a joyful encounter, that

every heart which adores You can unite completely with You, that all those who adore may be one in You just as You are one with the Father and the Holy Spirit. I adore You also in those churches and oratories where Your people have forgotten You and left You alone.

May Your Spirit be poured out on those parish communities where souls have not yet woken up to Adoration. They will come and adore You when You release Your Spirit, when the Spirit leads Your faithful into the mystery of Your presence.

- I adore You in the name of all those who have forgotten You!
(Repeat this prayer quietly within yourself)

8) Jesus, I thank You that You have remained with us in the Eucharistic bread and wine. I glorify You with my whole soul. Together with all the angels and saints, I sing a hymn of thanksgiving.

I know, Lord, that even today You are scorned and held in contempt. I know that there are black masses and rituals where they tread on You and mortify You. I know that Satanist sects exist where their members try to obtain consecrated hosts for evil purposes to crush Your love.

Jesus, I present now to You my time, my love, my devotion, my deepest respect, my songs of praise and thanksgiving in reparation for sin and for the wounds and offenses which You constantly endure. I wish to defend You with my love, I want to be close to You.

- O Jesus, receive my love in reparation for all the offenses!
(Repeat this prayer quietly within yourself)

9) Now, Jesus, I want to glorify You, together with
Your Church, singing this hymn of praise:
Tantum ergo sacramentum
Veneremur cernui:
Et antiquum documentum
Novo cedat ritui;
Praestat fides supplementum
Senswuum defectui

> *Come adore this wondrous presence,*
> *Bow to Christ, the source of grace,*
> *Here is kept the ancient promise*
> *Of God's earthly dwelling place.*
> *Sight is blind before God's glory,*
> *Faith alone may see his face.*

Genitori Genitoque
Lacus et jubilation,
Salus, honor, virtus quoque
Sit et benediction;
Procedenti ab utroque
Compar sit laudation. Amen.

> *Glory be to God, the Father,*
> *Praise to His co-equal Son,*
> *Adoration to the Spirit,*
> *Bond of love in Godhead one.*
> *Blest be God by all creation*
> *Joyously while ages run. Amen.*

10) Blessing

Jesus, Holy Lord, I believe in Your love for the sick and for sinners. Before approaching You at the Eucharistic table, I say, together with the Church, "Lord, say only the Word and my soul shall be healed." So Lord, heal my soul, my faith, my love and my hope. Calm my heart and free it from all anxiety. Deliver me from all tension and fear and all that causes them to develop within me. Protect me from the deceptions of Satan. Protect our families, the Church and the world. Be glorified in the sick and the overburdened.

(Name those for whom you wish to pray)

Be praised and blessed now and forever in the Most Holy Sacrament of the Altar. Amen.

JESUS, TEACH ME TO PRAY (I)

1) I come to You, Jesus, and I adore You because
You are my teacher:
I love You because You have the word of eternal
life.
I believe in You because You are divine truth.

2) Jesus, I adore You and I wish to remain with You.
Thank You, Jesus, because not only did You invite Your
disciples to pray, but You Yourself prayed continually . In
every situation, You called upon the Father and the Holy
Spirit, You gave them thanks and glory.

Thank You because You took time to pray. You
wandered in lonely places. You went out into the
wilderness to pray. Thank You because I know that You
rose early, while it was still dark and went out on the hills
to pray. Before Your death, You prayed on the hill of
Gethsemane and even on the cross, You prayed. You
prayed before every miracle. Before every meal, You
blessed the bread, thanking the Father that He listened to
You.

- My Jesus, thank You for having always prayed.
(Repeat this prayer quietly within yourself)

3) Jesus, before You chose Your disciples, those who
would one day go out into the world to preach the gospel,
to heal the sick and to cast out demons, You prayed. St.
Luke tells us in his Gospel:

*"Now it happened in those days that He went onto the
mountains to pray; and He spent the whole night in prayer to God.*

When day came, He summoned and picked out twelve of them; He called them 'apostles'.'" (Lk 6:12-13)

Before every important decision, You prayed.

Lord Jesus, I wish to learn to pray. From now on, I want to do that too. Forgive me that I am often without prayer. I have made decisions for my future and made plans without consulting with the Father in the Holy Spirit. For this reason, I have often lost my way following my own desires. From now on, I promise to pray before every decision, to be illuminated and to try to discover the Father's will. I take back all those decisions that I made without You, where I sought only my own will, and I place myself under the will of the Father. From now on, may things be different in me. I want to be like You. Do not let haste push me nor pride and selfishness guide me. May Your Spirit guide me in everything – and may I be inspired by Your example.

- Jesus, teach me to seek the Father's will!
   (Repeat this invocation quietly within yourself)

4) Lord Jesus, You educated Your disciples with love and patience. You prayed with them. You showed Your divine beauty and Your divine origins by presenting the law of prayer. St Matthew tells us:

"Six days later, Jesus took with Him Peter and James and his brother John and led them up a high mountain by themselves. There in their presence, He was transfigured. His face shone like the sun and His clothes became as dazzling as light. And suddenly, Moses and Elijah appeared to them; they were talking with Him. Then Peter spoke to Jesus. "Lord," he said, "it is wonderful for us to be here. If You want me to, I will make three shelters here, one for You, one for Moses, and one for Elijah." He was still speaking,

when suddenly a bright cloud covered them with shadow, and suddenly from the cloud there came a voice that said: "This is my Son, the Beloved; he enjoys my favor. Listen to Him." When they heard this, the disciples fell on their faces overcome with fear. But Jesus came up and touched them, saying, "Stand up, do not be afraid." (Mt 17: 1-7)

Jesus, teach me to pray. Grant that I encounter the beauty of Your face, so that my whole being – my spirit, my soul and my heart – will say: It is good for me to be here. Forgive me, Jesus , that I have often felt prayer to be something long-drawn-out and boring, without joy and without love. Show me Your face so that, from now on, my prayer becomes a joyful dwelling with You. Forgive me that I have put up my tent and dwelt so far away from Your face. From now on, I want to be happy with You.

- Jesus, together with Peter, I repeat: It is good for me to be here with You!
(*Repeat this prayer quietly within yourself*)

5) Jesus, while You patiently taught Your Apostles to pray, there was one heart which, like Yours, continually prayed. That heart was the heart of Your and our mother, Mary. She wanted always to be with You. She always testified to Your divine splendor. Thank You for having sent Mary to invite me and to teach me to pray:

"Dear Children! Also today, I am inviting you to prayer. I am always inviting you, but you are still far away. Therefore, from today on, decide seriously to dedicate time to God. I am with you and I wish to teach you to pray with the heart. In the prayer with the heart, you shall encounter God. Therefore, little

children, pray, pray, pray! Thank you for having responded to my call." (October 25, 1989)

Mary, thank You that You are here in Adoration together with me and that you are teaching me to pray during this time. By Your intercession, may the Lord Jesus send the Spirit of Prayer into my heart. Do not let my heart remain hard, my ears deaf or my eyes blind.

- Jesus, teacher of prayer, teach me to pray with my heart like Mary.

(Repeat this invocation quietly within yourself)

6) Lord Jesus, Your Apostles observed how You continually prayed and, within their hearts, a desire to pray awoke. St Luke writes:

"Now it happened that He was in a certain place praying and when He had finished, one of His disciples said: "Lord, teach us to pray, as John taught his disciples." He said to them, when you pray, this is what to say: 'Father, may Your name be held holy, Your kingdom come; give us each day our daily bread, and forgive us our sins, for we ourselves forgive each one who is in debt to us. And do not put us to the test." (Lk 11:1-4)

- O Jesus, awake in me an ardent desire to pray!

(Repeat this invocation quietly within yourself)

7) Jesus, You told Your Apostles how to pray and how they had to improve their prayer. St Matthew writes:

"And when you pray, do not imitate the hypocrites: they love to say their prayers standing upright in the synagogue and at the street corners for people to see them. In truth I tell you they have had their reward. But when you pray, go to your private room, shut yourself in, and so pray to your Father who is in that secret place, and your Father, who sees all that is done in secret will reward you.

In your prayer, do not babble as the gentiles do, for they think that by using many words they will make themselves heard. Do not be like them, your Father knows what you need before you ask Him." (Mt 6:5-8)

How many times has my prayer been empty, with many words but no heart; and how many times have I prayed like a hypocrite, with neither heart nor love; but just so that others would see me. Jesus, forgive me, purify my heart, purify my intentions.

- Jesus, grant that my prayer is neither hypocritical nor pagan, but that it is prayer of the heart!
(Repeat this prayer quietly within yourself)

8) Jesus, You taught Your disciples to pray and You sent them into the world to continue Your work. I bless and thank You for every moment they spent teaching others to pray just as You had taught them. Thank You for all those who today continue Your work which was passed down to them by the Apostles. Pour out Your Spirit of prayer on the Pope, on bishops, priests, religious and consecrated people, on parents and catechists so that they can pray for others and teach others to pray. May they no longer wish to pray only with their lips, leaving their hearts far away from You. And may they no longer excuse themselves saying that they have no time, when really they have no faith nor love for You.

- Unleash Your Spirit of prayer in the hearts of Your faithful!
(Repeat this invocation quietly within yourself)

9) Jesus, be blessed in all those who wish to pray, who take time for personal prayer in families, in prayer groups and in Your Church. Grant that they make progress along the spiritual path and that they can always feel how near You are through prayer. May they mature spiritually. Protect them from temptation and from evil. Protect them from spiritual pride or from the contempt and scorn of others. Grant that they get to know You better through prayer and that they open themselves to the Holy Spirit. May prayer become their joy.

Bless also those who pray but never see any progress and, consequently, tire and doubt the importance of their prayer. Bless those who are already steeped in the depths of prayer too. May Your Spirit guide and look after them.

- Jesus, increase the number of people who pray in Your Church and take care of them on their spiritual path!
(*Repeat this invocation quietly within yourself*)

10) Blessing

Jesus, You said that whoever prayed in Your name with faith would be listened to. I believe in Your words. That is why I pray: Heal the spirit of prayer in my heart, may Your Spirit continually pray within me. Remove from me, all that is blocking me from praying with my heart. Heal the spirit of prayer in our families, in the communities and in the Church. Unleash Your Spirit of prayer and listen to us. Heal us in body and soul. Heal all the sick and disabled. May Your name be glorified among us. Grant us Your peace, You who live and reign world without end. Amen.

JESUS, TEACH ME TO PRAY (II)

1) Jesus, I adore You because You are the One true God.
   I believe in You because You are the One true truth.
   I love You because You are my teacher.

2) Thank You that I can be with You again and that, with You, I can learn to pray. Thank You because You have endless time for me. I thank You because I know where to find You. I thank You that You have inflamed my heart with a yearning to get to know You better and, with You, to get to know the Father better. I know that this can happen only when You send me Your Holy Spirit. Send Him, Lord, in His fullness so that my heart and soul and everything in me immerse in Your Eucharistic presence and remain there. You too invite me to pray continually. And responding to my question, "How can I do this?" St. Paul writes:

"So then, my brothers, we have no obligation to human nature to be dominated by it. If you do live in that way, you are doomed to die; but if by the Spirit you put to death the habits originating in the body, you will have life. All who are guided by the Spirit of God are sons of God; for what you received was not a spirit of slavery to bring you back into fear; you received the spirit of adoption, enabling us to cry out: "Abba, Father!" The Spirit himself bears witness that we are children of God. ...And as well as this, the Spirit too comes to help us in our weakness, for, when we do not know how to pray properly, then the Spirit personally makes our petitions for us in groans that cannot be put into words, ..."
(Rom 8:12-16, 26)

- Jesus, may Your Spirit continually pray within me: "Abba, Father!"
(Repeat this prayer quietly within yourself)

3) Lord Jesus, Mary's whole heart, in its infinite wisdom and motherly yearnings, remained always immersed in that Spirit, which protected Her from sin and from every fault. She invites and teaches me:

"Dear children! Also today, I want to call you all to prayer. Let prayer be your life. Dear children, dedicate your time only to Jesus and He will give you everything you are seeking. He will reveal Himself to you in fullness. Dear children, Satan is strong and is waiting to test each one of you. Pray, and, that way, he will neither be able to injure you nor block you on the way of holiness. Dear children, through prayer, grow all the more towards God from day to day. Thank you for having responded to my call."
(September 25, 1987)

- Jesus, reveal Yourself in Your fullness to my heart, so that my life becomes a prayer.
(Repeat this prayer quietly within yourself)

4) Jesus, with You and in the Holy Spirit, I now wish to repeat in the silence of my heart the words which You gave the Apostles when they asked You to teach them to pray. Grant that my heart finds peace in you and may Your Spirit act within me. Make my heart be like Your Mother's. May my soul sing in prayer.

- Jesus, fill me with Your presence and become the beloved One of my heart!
(Repeat this invocation quietly within yourself)

(We now pray the Our Father, slowly repeating every prayer once. If doing group Adoration, a verse could be sung between each prayer)

5) Our Father who art in Heaven!

6) Hallowed be Your name, may Your kingdom come.

7) May Your will be done on earth as it is in Heaven.

8) Give us this day our daily bread!

9) Forgive us our trespasses as we forgive those who trespass against us!

10) And lead us not into temptation but deliver us from evil!

11) Blessing

Jesus, teacher, bless me with Your Spirit of Prayer. Purify my heart, my soul and my intentions. Forgive me that I am so slow to understand and that the things of this world take me in so easily. Forgive me that I so easily found excuses why I could not pray. Forgive me that prayer was so hard for me. Heal me, body and soul, protect me from evil.

Bless, protect and heal all those for whom I pray. Deliver our families, communities, the Church and the world from evil. May Your kingdom come within them forever, in Your Holy Spirit who lives and reigns together with You and the Father forever and ever. Amen.

JESUS, YOU ARE ALIVE, ALLELUIA!

1) I adore You, Jesus, because You have the victory over death.
I love You because You overcame sin through love.
I believe in You, Jesus, because You are risen.

2) Blessed be that moment, three days after Your death, when You gloriously arose. Blessed be that glorious moment when Your cold grave was left empty and that grave stone no longer protected a body. Blessed be that moment when the sunrise of the resurrection dawned on this world. May my heart sing and rejoice, and my soul jubilate and applaud. May the angels and saints, together with all creation, unite in singing Your praises because You have the victory over death and You are alive.

— Jesus, I exalt in Your glorious resurrection. Alleluia!
(Repeat this prayer quietly within yourself)

3) Jesus, blessed be that renowned and happy moment when You came to Your Mother, Mary. Because of Her motherly love, Her suffering was almost as great as Your own. And when everyone had lost hope, She continued to hope because, in Her heart, She had nurtured Your words and the words which had been prophesied and said about You. What a glorious moment when You appeared and said, "Peace be with You, Mother."

Mary, thank You that, in faith, in hope and in love, with total abandonment, You awaited that moment of joyful togetherness after the Resurrection. You wish for my heart to open and rejoice too; that is why at Easter time, You exclaimed:

"Dear children! Rejoice with me! Alleluia, alleluia, alleluia!" (Easter 1987)

- Mary, I want to celebrate the victory of love and life with You. Alleluia!

(Repeat this prayer quietly within yourself)

4) Jesus, blessed be that moment when, in fear and deep sorrow, the women went to find You at dawn. They did not know that You awaited them alive. They did not imagine that the gravestone could have been moved. They even asked themselves how they would move it because it was too heavy for them. It had already been accomplished!

"Mary Magdalene remained outside the grave, crying. Then, while she cried, her gaze fell upon the open grave where two angels were sitting; one at the point where the head of Jesus had been and one at the foot. They said to her: "Woman, why are you weeping?" "They have taken my Lord away," She replied, "and I do not know where they have put him." As she said this, she turned round and saw Jesus standing there, although she did not realize that it was Jesus. Jesus said to her: "Woman, why are you weeping? Who are you looking for?" Supposing Him to be the gardener, she said: "Sir, if you have taken him away, tell me where you have put him, and I will go and remove him." Jesus said: "Mary!" She turned round and said to Him in Hebrew 'Rabbuni' which means Master." (Jn 20:13-16)

\-   Rabunni, my teacher, You are alive. Alleluia!
(Repeat this prayer quietly within yourself)

5) Jesus, my Lord, You have arisen from the dead and blessed be that moment when You appeared to Your disciples. Your death frightened them. In their terror, they had gathered together awaiting whatever was to happen to them. St. John writes:

"In the evening of that same day, the first day of the week, the doors were closed in the room where the disciples were, for fear of the Jews. Jesus came and stood among them. He said to them, 'Peace be with you,' and, after saying this, He showed them His hands and His side. The disciples were filled with joy at seeing the Lord, and He said to them again, 'Peace be with you.'"
(Jn 20:19-20)

Thank You for that blessed moment when, at the sound of Your voice, peace returned to their hearts, their faces were resplendent with joy and they were delivered from their fears.

\-   O Jesus, I rejoice with Your Apostles at Your Resurrection. Alleluia!
(Repeat this prayer quietly within yourself)

6) Jesus, risen Lord, I adore You and thank You for meeting with Your two disciples on the road from Jerusalem to Emmaus. They were returning home, disheartened. All their hopes had been buried together with Your dead body on Good Friday. Thank You for explaining and interpreting the Scriptures to them, because after that their hearts began to burn. The resurrection began for them when You put hope back into their hearts.

Thank You for remaining with them, for opening their eyes so that they could recognize You. St. Luke writes:

'When they drew near to the village to which they were going, He made as if to go on; but they pressed Him to stay with them saying: 'It is nearly evening, and the day is almost over.' So He went in to stay with them. Now while He was with them at the table, He took the bread and said the blessing, then He broke it and handed it to them. And their eyes were opened and they recognized Him; but He had vanished from their sight. Then they said to each other: 'Did not our hearts burn within us as He talked to us on the road and explained the scriptures to us?'"(Lk 24:28-32)

- Open my eyes! May my heart burn, Jesus, because You are alive. Alleluia!
  (Repeat this invocation quietly within yourself)

7) Lord Jesus, be blessed for all those who opened their hearts and believed immediately. Be blessed in those who had questions, who expressed doubts and set up conditions by which they would concede to believe. St. John writes:

'Thomas, called the twin, who was one of the twelve, was not with them when Jesus came. So the other disciples said to him: 'We have seen the Lord.' But he answered: 'Unless I can see the holes that the nails made in His hands and can put my finger into the holes they made, and unless I can put my hand into the hole in His side, I refuse to believe.' ...the doors were closed, but Jesus came in and stood among them. 'Peace be with you.' He said. Then He spoke to Thomas: 'Put your finger here; look, here are my hands. Give me your hand; put it into my side. Do not be unbelieving anymore but believe.' Thomas replied: 'My Lord and my God.'" (Jn 20: 24-8)

- Together with Thomas, I jubilantly proclaim You, "My Lord and my God."
(Repeat this prayer quietly within yourself)

8) Lord Jesus, be blessed, because You have arisen from the dead and have restored peace and hope to Your disciples. Your death had thrown them into the darkness of fear, hopelessness and disbelief, losing the very will to live and that necessary trust in one another. Risen Jesus, meet and remain with those who, like the two from Emmaus, are shaken by sadness and tragedy, and have neither life nor hope left within them. Especially, meet and remain with the young. Open up their hearts to the Scriptures, let them recognize and glorify You.
(Now present in your hear those who you know are going through trials in the depths of their souls)

9) Lord Jesus, come today to all sick and disabled persons, come to the lonely, the handicapped children and to those who, through debilitating diseases, are in danger of losing hope and their ability to love. Come to those who help them and who work with them. Show them Your glorified wounds, Your open side-wound and open their hearts during their suffering. May they believe that all suffering will turn into glory.
(Now present all the sick people you know!)

10) Blessing

Jesus, You are alive! I believe this. I beg You now to put Your glorified right hand into every wound in our bodies and in our souls and to heal us. Touch with Your love all that is contaminated with the stain of deadly sin. Open those hearts which are now like graves, and save families where love, peace and joy are buried beneath the seed of sin. Give new life to communities, to the Church and to the world. May they unite in glorifying Your Resurrection, because You live and reign world without end. Amen.

KEEP WATCH WITH ME

1) Lord Jesus, here I am now with You. When You asked the Apostles to keep watch and pray with You so that they would not fall into temptation, You were asking me too. Thank You that, with Your Spirit, You have awakened in me a desire to be with You and praise Your love with which You burned, desiring to give Yourself to us. Drive far from me all that is hindering me from being with You. Free me from all tiredness so that I can keep watch with You. I wish to rest my heart on Your sweet and blessed chest, and hear the beat of Your noble heart in those moments when You were at the table with Your disciples, when You gave us Your body and when You prayed in the garden of Gethsemane.

- Free me, Jesus, from all that is hindering me from being with You!
(Repeat this invocation quietly within yourself)

2) Jesus, Lord, the time of Your passion is the time of Your glory. You prayed:
"Father the hour has come. Glorify Your Son so that Your Son may glorify You; so that, just as You have given Him power over all humanity, He may give eternal life to all those You have entrusted to Him. And eternal life is this: to know You, the only true God, and Jesus Christ whom You have sent. I have glorified You on earth by finishing the work that You gave me to do. Now, Father, glorify me with that glory I had with You before ever the world existed... But now I am coming to You and I say these things in the world to share my joy with them to the full!" (Jn 17:1b-5;13)

71

I admit, Jesus, that it is so hard for me to see that the moment of Your passion is the moment of glory. This mystery is hidden from my eyes, but deep in my heart I know that it is true.

- Father, the hour has come! Glorify Your Son!
(Repeat this prayer quietly within yourself)

3) Jesus, in my thoughts now, I want to be with You from the time of Your last supper with the disciples and on the road to the Mount of Olives. How You must have felt in Your heart and Your soul as You made communion with Your disciples, giving them Your very body and blood! I want to be with You. Did Your Apostles realize that this was the moment of glory in which Your suffering would begin? St. Luke writes:

"When He reached the place, He said to them: 'Pray not to be put to the test.' Then He withdrew from them about a stones throw away, and knelt down and prayed. 'Father,' He said, 'if You are willing, take this cup away from me. Nevertheless, let Your will, not mine be done.'" (Lk 22:40b-42)

- Father, let Your will and not mine be done, now and forever!
(Repeat this invocation quietly within yourself)

4) Jesus, while You prayed alone, Your heart was joined to that of Your Mother, Mary. She felt everything and lived through every moment together with You, even though She was not physically present. Your hearts were deeply united with an inexpressible bond of love. On Good Friday, She invited me with few and frank words:

"Dear children! Sympathize with me! Pray, pray, pray!" (April 19, 1984)

Thank You, Mary, that You suffered together with Your Son that evening. Now I want to do what You invited me to in Your message. Through Your intercession, may the Lord purify my heart from any hard-heartedness and lack of feeling. Fill my heart with Your feelings, Mary. I want to share Your sentiments now like a little child who sympathizes with its Mother.

> - O, Mary, I want to share Your sentiments and be close to Jesus.
> *(Repeat this prayer quietly within yourself)*

5) Jesus, the Apostles heard Your call in the garden of Gethsemane, but they were physically exhausted and fell asleep. St. Matthew tells us:

> *"He came back to the disciples and found them sleeping and he said to Peter: 'So you had not the strength to stay awake with me for one hour? Stay awake, and pray not to be put to the test. The spirit is willing enough, but human nature is weak.'"* (Mt 26:40-41)

Jesus, how it must have hurt You when You saw that the Apostles had fallen asleep, when they had not noticed the agony You were going through and just gave in to drowsiness, while You, on Your knees, were experiencing deathly fear. You admonish them and invite them once again to prayer, but You did not judge them. The heart was willing but the flesh was weak.

> - Jesus, make my spirit ready, and deliver me from the weakness of the flesh and I will be with You!
> *(Repeat this invocation quietly within yourself)*

6) Jesus, Your Apostles heard You asking them to keep watch with You but, sadly, out of tiredness, they fell asleep. St Matthew writes:

"And He came back again and found them sleeping, their eyes were so heavy. Leaving them there, He went away again and prayed for the third time, repeating the same words." (Mt 26:43-44)

My Jesus, this time you did not even waken Your disciples, instead You continued to pray alone, to suffer and to agonize alone. How great is Your love for Your disciples and for us, O Jesus! How great is Your goodness and how deep is Your humility! You are not angry because the Apostles are sleeping, You do not reproach them for their insensitivity, their weakness or laziness, You just continue to pray. I praise You and bless You because I continually rediscover Your love and Your mercy. I desire deeply to remain here and keep watch with You. Thank You because You do not ask where have I been until now. Thank You that You do not reject me for having thrown away precious time occupying myself pointlessly. Thank You that You do not bring up my faults, but permit me to remain with You just as I am.

- Jesus, grant that my keeping vigil with You may be a sign of my love.
(Repeat this prayer quietly within yourself)

7) Jesus, this night is mysterious! You abandon Yourself to the Father and Your disciples abandon You out of tiredness. You suffer and pray, You sweat blood and offer Yourself up to the Father. The only one who is keeping watch and who is not overcome by sleep is Judas,

the traitor. He does not sleep. He prepares his betrayal and arrives with his colleagues to take You while You are engrossed in prayer. Even when seeing all this, piercing pain cuts through Your heart, You still continue to love! St. Matthew writes:

"Now the traitor had arranged a sign with them saying: 'The one I kiss, He is the man. Arrest Him.' So he went up to Jesus at once and said: 'Greetings, Rabbi.' And kissed Him. Jesus said to him: ' My friend, do what you are here for..'" (Mt 26:46-50a)

O Jesus, even though I am taken aback by Your betrayer's behavior, Your reaction surprises me! In that moment of betrayal when that word of greeting was used to hand You over, You find the inner strength to address Judas as "friend!" This was really what You felt coming face to face with him. My heart is in love with You, Jesus. My soul marvels at such love, which overcomes every suggestion to be negative, which is neither disturbed nor influenced by our attitudes.

(Remain in silence meditating upon this)

8) I adore You, Lord Jesus, tonight, together with those throughout the whole world, who have gone out to pray, to adore You, who offer You their love and their thanks. I thank You, together with all those who return Your love with love and are inspired by this, all those praying alone, all prayer groups, communities who have night-long vigils with You. May they be filled with love and peace and a deep unity with You and Your Mother Mary. May many hearts be inspired and make reparation for all those who sleep, who betray You, who while enslaved to this world spend night and day in evil and sin,

drugs and alcohol, and who consequently betray their families, fathers and mothers, husbands and wives. I pray for all those who do ill to others.

- Jesus, may their spirits be stronger than the weakness of the flesh and may they be delivered from evil!

(Repeat this prayer quietly within yourself)

9) Jesus, tonight many are alone in their pain, abandoned by the ones they love, living their own private Gethsemanes, and there is no one to comfort them. Many are called to leave this world tonight un-reconciled with others and un-reconciled with their heavenly Father. Thank You for the gift of being able to pray for them so that they feel Your closeness, and that You send Your angels to comfort them.

(Present to Him by name those who you know are suffering, and those who are with them or should be with them.)

10) Blessing

My Jesus, bless me, my family, my friends, my enemies, all those for whom You suffered, and grant that Your love unite us, calm us and protect us. May we continually glorify Your love. Take all our personal struggles and sorrow and unite them with Your blood and sweat. Offer them to the Father for the salvation of the world. May all those who have not yet said, "Not my, but Thy will be done" receive the strength tonight to do so. May You be glorified in them, You who live and reign world without end. Amen.

JESUS, I PRAISE YOU
FOR YOUR MERCY (I)

1) I adore You, Jesus, because You are full of mercy. I love You, Jesus, because You came to forgive. I believe in You because You came to make me whole in body and soul.

2) Jesus, in You the Father demonstrated His infinite love to us, who are sick in body and soul. For this, I wish to thank You, to praise You, to glorify and to bless You. You are my God and my Savior. Thank You for these words of St. Matthew:

"Now while He was at table in the house it happened that a number of tax-collectors and sinners came to sit at the table with Jesus and His disciples. When the Pharisees saw this, they said to His disciples: 'Why does your mast eat with tax-collectors and sinners?' When He heard this He replied: 'It is not the healthy who need the doctor, but the sick. Go and learn the meaning of the words: Mercy is what pleases me, not sacrifice. And indeed I came to call not the upright but sinners.'" (Mt 9:10-13)

O Jesus, my heart feels deeply the magnitude of Your love and mercy in these, Your words. Thank You, Jesus, because You were not afraid to sit at the table with tax collectors and sinners. Especially because, for the Pharisees, this itself was a sin and a violation of the law. But, Your love was not influenced by this.

- Jesus, I adore You, because You love mercy more than sacrifice.
(Repeat this prayer quietly within yourself)

3) My Jesus, I adore You, together with Mary, Your and our Mother. I call Her the Mother of Mercy and I give honor to Her because She gave birth to You who are mercy personified. She was with You from birth, and She knows of the Father's mercy and patience towards us sinners.

Thank You, Mary, because You too call us with great patience and You, as a mother, warn us. You come to us daily and remain with us so long to help us understand the Father's mercy that was demonstrated by Your Son. Thank You for having said:

"Dear children! ...I love you, dear children, and that is why I have been calling you – I do not know how many times – and thank you for all that you are doing for my intentions. I beg you, help me to present you to God, to save you and to lead you on the way of salvation. Thank you for having responded to my call." (June 25, 1987)

- Jesus, I adore You, together with Mary, the Mother of Mercy.
  (*Repeat this prayer quietly within yourself*)

4) Jesus, Infinite Mercy, thank You for having thought of the tired and the overburdened. Your mercy was especially intended for these. St. Matthew writes:

"Come to me all who labour and are heavy burdened, and I will give you rest. Shoulder my yoke and learn from me, for I am gentle and humble in heart, and you will find rest for your souls. Yes, my yoke is easy and my burden is light." (Mt 11:28-30)

Jesus, I come to You with all my suffering and trials, my crosses and everything that is weighing me down. I remain here in front of You because, in Your mercy, You accept me as I am. I am so tired, Jesus, because what I am carrying within me is exhausting me. My sins and my imperfections torture me and I am worn out judging and condemning myself and others. My relationship with this world, with myself and with others, is tiring me. I am tired and heavy burdened but I am counting on Your mercy and help.

- Here I am, O Jesus, tired and heavy burdened.
  (*Repeat this prayer quietly within yourself*)

5) Jesus, I can now sing in my soul because I can hand over to You all that is bothering me. O, how great is Your love and mercy towards me! I can come to You because, even when I am depressing and hard company for myself and others, I am never a burden for You. O, how beautiful it is to spend time with You! O Jesus, You are so meek and humble of heart that You give rest to my weary soul. Together with the Psalmist, I wish to sing:

"I will bless Yahweh at all times, His praise continually on my lips.
I will praise Yahweh from my heart; let the humble hear and rejoice.
Proclaim with me the greatness of Yahweh, let us acclaim His name together.
I seek Yahweh and He answers me, frees me from all my fears.
Fix your gaze upon Yahweh and your face will grow bright, you will never hang your head in shame.
A pauper calls out Yahweh hears, saves him from all his troubles.
The angel of Yahweh encamps around those who fear Him and rescues them.
Taste and see that Yahweh is good.
How blessed are those who take refuge in Him.
Fear Yahweh, you His holy ones; those who fear Him lack for nothing.

Young lions may go needy and hungry, but those who seek Yahweh lack nothing good." (Ps 34:1-11)

- May my soul bless and praise Your name Jesus.
(*Repeat this prayer quietly within yourself*)

6) Jesus, how beautiful it is to be bathed in the light of Your beautiful face; how beautiful it is to be near Your merciful heart; how easy it is to look in to those eyes which radiate mercy and forgiveness and how easy it is to rest myself on that heart which is meek, humble and profoundly good!

Jesus, I want to bring before You now all those times when I was merciless with myself, when I was not attentive to the needs of my soul, my heart or my body, when I judged myself, when I did not know how to forgive myself, when I did not listen to Your voice within me. How many times, Jesus, after having sinned, my pride got the better of me, and I could not accept or believe in Your forgiveness and mercy. Be blessed, praised and glorified, Jesus, for Your real presence in the Eucharist. It is a sign that I am still important to You. You remained with me, so that the Father's mercy could be a foundation for my forgiveness and mercy towards others.

- Forgive my merciless heart for its treatment of myself and others.
(*Repeat this prayer quietly within yourself*)

7) Thank You, Jesus, that You told Your disciples to forgive sinners in Your name and to welcome them as You welcomed them. Be blessed in Your Apostles

because, in Your name, they did what You said and they passed down the gifts to their successors. Be blessed in the Pope, in bishops and in all priests and confessors who, in Your name, in the sacrament of reconciliation, forgive sins, showing every sinner the goodness and mercy of the Father. Be blessed in all those priests who, like You, have become a reflection of the Father's mercy. Bless them, Jesus, and give them strength that they continually and zealously be humble servants of Your mercy. Be blessed also in those who have become lukewarm or who are impatient and avoid the confessionals. Fill them with Your Spirit and may every priestly heart become meek and humble like Your own.

(In silence, pray for your confessor and for all those who come to confess to him, and for all who have had a bad experience at confession.)

8) Jesus, how beautiful it was for You, Mary and Joseph, because divine mercy prevailed among You. How much goodness, love, forgiveness, understanding and humility prevailed among You in Your holy family!

Be blessed, Jesus, in those parents who show mercy to each other and to their children and, in that way, create happiness and togetherness. Consolidate them in their love. Be blessed also in those families where there is no more mercy, where parents offend and insult each other, where they have no respect for one another, and so transmit their unhappiness to their children who suffer and are tormented, and who will bear the wounds throughout their whole lives. Be blessed because it is You who will open their eyes and help them to live with mercy, thereby glorifying the merciful Father.

(In silence, think of your family and of other families you know and pray for them.)

9) Jesus, be blessed for all the mercy to be found in the world; I praise You for all those good and merciful people and movements who pass through the world doing good. Bless them, Lord, and increase Your mercy in the world by pouring it into their hearts.

You know, Jesus, how little mercy and how much cruelty there is in the world, how easily unborn and even born lives are taken, how easily families and communities are destroyed, how much cruelty and mercilessness there is among young people with drugs, alcohol, and immoral behavior which brings them to their ruin. How many are overwhelmed by a spirit of violence and destruction. Thank You, Jesus, that You have not abandoned us, You still come not to judge us but to save us. Forgive me that I have often judged and rejected those whom I considered to be sinners. Instead of helping them, I dared to look down on them and judge them! I now invoke Your mercy for all.

(In silence, pray, mentioning people, places and nations where un-mercifulness reigns!)

10) Blessing

Merciful Jesus, have mercy on me, on my family, my friends and acquaintances, the sick and the sinners. Have mercy on this world!

Protect and heal in body and soul every person and every relationship between people and between nations. Make the heart of every person like Your own, You who live and reign, and show mercy world without end. Amen.

82

JESUS, I PRAISE YOU
FOR YOUR MERCY (II)

(These prayers are especially suitable during the Novena to Divine Mercy from Good Friday to the Sunday after Easter.)

1) I adore You, Jesus, because You are immeasurably merciful.
I love You, Jesus, because, in Your eyes, mercy is sweeter than sacrifice.
I believe in You, Jesus, because You have revealed the merciful Father to me.

2) I adore You, Jesus, together with Mary, the Mother of Mercy, because She was the very first to experience Your mercy. From Her conception, You had already saved Her from sin and its consequences. I wish to praise the mercy of the Father, together with You, because it was manifested in such a marvelous way in Your life. I greet You now because You are here with me just at You promised.

> I greet You, Holy Queen, Mother of Mercy:
> *Hail our life, our sweetness and our hope,*
> *to Thee do we cry poor banished children of Eve,*
> *to Thee do we send up our sighs;*
> *mourning and weeping in this valley of tears.*
> *Turn then, most gracious advocate,*
> *Your eyes of mercy towards us,*
> *And, after this, our exile,*
> *Show unto us the blessed fruit of Your womb,*
> *O clement,*

O loving,
O sweet virgin Mary
Pray for us, O Holy Mother of God,
That we may be made worthy of the
Promises of Christ.

-      Jesus, I adore You, together with the Queen of
Mercy!
      (Repeat this prayer quietly within yourself)

   3)   Jesus, I thank You because, in your goodness and
mercy, You returned to Zacchaeus' house. St Luke writes:
      "He entered Jericho and was going through the town and
suddenly a man whose name was Zacchaeus made his appearance; he
was one of the senior tax-collectors and a wealthy man. He kept
trying to see which one Jesus was, but he was too short and could not
see him for the crowd; so he ran ahead and climbed a sycamore tree to
catch a glimpse of Jesus who was to pass that way. When Jesus
reached the spot, He looked up and spoke to him: 'Zacchaeua; come
down. Hurry because I am to stay at your house today.' And he
hurried down and welcomed Him joyfully. They all complained when
they saw what was happening. 'He has gone to stay at a sinners
house,' they said. But Zacchaeus stood his ground and said to the
Lord: 'Look, sir, I am going to give half my property to the poor,
and if I have cheated anybody, I will pay him back four times the
amount.' And Jesus said to him: 'Today salvation has come to this
house, because this man too is a son of Abraham; for the Son of man
has come to seek out and save what was lost.'" (Lk 19:1-10)

-      Jesus, come in Your mercy and save what is
lost!
(Repeat this prayer quietly within yourself)

4) Jesus, thank You for not rejecting the repentant and humble tax-collector from the synagogue, instead You justified him:

"The tax-collector stood some distance away, not daring even to raise his eyes to Heaven; but he beast his breast and said: 'God, be merciful to me, a sinner.' This man, I tell you, went home again justified; the other did not. For everyone who raises himself up will be humbled, but he who humbles himself will be raised up.'" (Lk 18:13-14)

- Merciful Jesus, I adore You, "have mercy on me, a sinner!"

(Repeat this prayer quietly within yourself)

5) Jesus, I bless You and thank You, because You revealed the good and merciful Father to me. You speak about the two sons – one of them leaves his family, spends all and returns. And the Father, in his mercy, yearns for his return, takes pity on him, runs to him, throws his arms around him and kisses him. And the Son says to him:

"Father, I have sinned against Heaven and against you, I no longer deserve to be called your son.' But the Father said to his servants: 'Quick! Bring out the best robe and put it on him; put a ring on his finger and sandals on his feet. Bring the calf we have been fattening, and kill it' we will celebrate by having a feast, because this son of mine was dead and has come back to life; he was lost and is found." (Lk 15:20b-24)

- Merciful Jesus, may parents feel mercy towards their children.

(Repeat this prayer quietly within yourself)

6) Jesus, the Pharisees were angry with You too for preaching mercy and for being merciful with sinners. You explained the Father's mercy to them. Their anger did not disturb You. You continued to reveal God's mercy. St. Luke writes:

"The tax-collectors and sinners, however, were all crowding around to listen to Him, and the Pharisees and scribes complained saying: 'This man welcomes sinners and eats with them.' So He told them this parable: 'Which one of you with a hundred sheep, if he lost one, would fail to leave the ninety-nine in the desert and go after the missing one till he found it? And when he found it, would he not joyfully take it on his shoulders and then, when he got home, call together his friends and neighbors, saying to them: 'Rejoice with me, I have found my sheep that was lost.'" (Lk 15:1-6)

- Merciful Jesus, bring all the lost back to the Father's house.
(Repeat this invocation quietly within yourself)

7) Jesus, in Your mercy and love towards Your own people, You even cried. St. Luke writes:

"As He drew near and came in sight of the city, He shed tears over it and said: 'If you too had only recognized on this day the way to peace! But in fact it is hidden from your eyes! Yes, a time is coming when your enemies will raise fortifications all around you, when they will encircle you and hem you in one every side; they will dash you and the children inside your walls to the ground; they will leave not one stone standing on another within you, because you did not recognize the moment of your visitation.'" (Lk 15:1-6)

- Merciful Jesus, grant that my people recognize the time of grace and convert!
(Repeat this prayer quietly within yourself)

8) Jesus, thank You for Your immeasurable mercy which I recognize in Your words, Your comparisons and in Your teachings. I remain now in silence before You, and I open myself up to Your mercy. May I be bathed in the light of Your face. I open myself up to You in the name of the whole world and I beg You:

-Jesus, have mercy on us.
(*Repeat this invocation quietly within yourself*)

9) Honoring the Divine Mercy, we now pray the Chaplet of Divine Mercy:

Our Father... Hail Mary... Apostles' Creed...
(*On the big beads:*)

Eternal Father, I offer You the body and blood, soul and divinity of Your dearly beloved Son, Our Lord Jesus Christ, in atonement for our sins and those of the whole world.

(*On the small beads:*)

For the sake of His sorrowful passion, have mercy on us and on the whole world.

(*After five decades, say three times:*)

Holy God, Holy mighty One, Holy Immortal One, have mercy on us and on the whole world.

10) Blessing

Jesus, pour out Your mercy upon us. Forgive us our sins, heal our wounds, free us from our bad habits, drive from us the spirit of mercilessness, violence and destruction. Shine upon us the blessed light of Your face and grant us Your peace. You who live and reign, world without end. Amen.

JESUS, SEND US YOUR HOLY SPIRIT (I)

(It is recommended that these prayers be prayed during the Novena to the Holy Spirit after the feast of the Ascension.)

1) Dwell within me Holy Spirit!
   Blaze up within me, Holy Spirit!
   Act within me Holy Spirit!

2) Jesus, I pray to You now, together with Mary and the Apostles, that, in these days, Your Holy Spirit will be poured out upon us, just at You promised. Mary and the Apostles prayed steadfastly together for nine days, and You fulfilled Your promise.

Thank You, Mary, that You will now pray with me and help me to persevere in prayer. You said:

"Dear children! Tonight I wish to tell you, during the days of this novena, to pray for the outpouring of the Holy Spirit on your families and on your parish. Pray, and you shall not regret it. God will give you gifts by which you will glorify Him till the end of your life on this earth. Thank you for having responded to my call." (June 2, 1984)

- Jesus, together with Mary, I beg You: send us Your Spirit!
  (Repeat this invocation quietly within yourself)

3) Jesus, send Your Spirit of love so that I am able to love just as You loved. You loved unconditionally. I know that, on the last day, You will ask me whether I loved, whether I recognized You in others and whether I loved them. I am not even conscious of how far away I

am from loving the way You love. That is why I am praying to You now:

- Jesus, pour out Your Spirit of love into my heart!

(Repeat this invocation quietly within yourself)

4) Jesus, send me Your Spirit of wisdom and knowledge. Send me that Spirit who wisely spoke through the prophets, through the Apostles and through every simple soul who praised and thanked You throughout the ages. I need true wisdom, and You are its source. I need it so that I can always discern Your path, recognize Your voice and realize Your plans. Send Your Spirit of wisdom on parents and all those who educate children, on teachers, tutors and professors, all those in politics, all those directing others, and all those commanding armies.

- Jesus, send me Your Spirit of wisdom and knowledge!

(Repeat this invocation quietly within yourself)

5) Jesus, Your Spirit has strengthened the weak. How easily I fall into sin, how easily temptations take control of me and how easily I put off doing good. How hard it is for me to forgive and to love. Send that Spirit of strength to men and women so that they persevere in a loving union. Send Your Spirit of strength to the young so that they can make a stand against the temptations of this world. Send it to the sick and the disabled, the distraught and the depressed, and all those who have lost their joy in living.

- Jesus, send Your Spirit of strength and fortify the weak!

(Repeat this invocation quietly within yourself)

6) Jesus, send me Your Spirit of counsel and discernment. There is so much disorder in the world. Many do not discern between good and evil and have no one who can give them counsel! How many live in conflict and unease, following the counsel of evil! Send Your Spirit of counsel to parents, teachers, doctors, preachers, and confessors.

- Jesus, send us Your Spirit of counsel and discernment!

(Repeat this invocation quietly within yourself)

7) Jesus, send Your Spirit of devotion and 'holy fear' into my heart and into the hearts of all people. We have become hardhearted and deaf to Your words. We lack a real and sincere relationship with You. Many are caught up with a spirit of atheism and materialism, they have become attached to this world and they will not make time for prayer. And when Your Spirit is not nourished within us, another spirit can enter – a spirit of abusive language, a spirit of lies and deception, a spirit of envy and jealousy, a spirit of disorder and distress, a spirit of violence and destruction, a spirit of unrepentance and pride, a spirit of hatred and refusal to reconcile, a spirit of laziness and excess in food and drink, a spirit of atheism and moral perversity.

- Jesus, send Your Spirit of devotion and 'holy fear!'

(Repeat this invocation quietly within yourself)

8) Together with the whole Church, I pray:
Come, Holy Spirit, Creator, come
From thy bright heavenly throne,

Come, take possession of our souls
And make them all thine own.

Thou who are called the Paraclete,
Best gift of God above,
The living spring, the living fire
Sweet unction and true love.

Thou who art sevenfold in thy grace,
Finger of God's right hand;
His promise, teaching little ones
To speak and understand

O guide our minds with thy blest light
With love our hearts inflame;
And with thy strength, which never decays,
Confirm our mortal frame.

Far from us drive our deadly foe;
True peace unto us bring;
And from all perils, lead us safe
Beneath thy sacred wing.

Through thee may we the Father know,
Through thee th'eternal Son
And thee the Spirit of them both,
Thrice blessed three in One.

All glory to the Father be
With his begotten Son;
The same to thee, great Paraclete
While endless ages run. Amen.

9) The Litany to the Holy Spirit:

Lord have mercy!
Christ have mercy!
Lord have mercy!
Christ hear us!
Christ graciously hear us!
God, our heavenly Father, have mercy on us!
God, the Son, Savior of the world, have mercy on us!
God, the Holy Spirit, have mercy on us!
Holy Trinity, One God, have mercy on us!

Spirit of the Father and the Son,	Come into our hearts!
Spirit of wisdom and knowledge,	"
Spirit of counsel and strength,	"
Spirit fo intellect and devotion,	Come into our hearts!
Spirit of holy fear,	"
Spirit of faith, hope and charity,	"
Spirit of joy and peace,	"
Spirit of humility and meekness,	"
Spirit of patience and modesty,	"
Spirit of purity and innocence,	"
Spirit of loyalty and transparency,	"
Spirit of holiness and justice,	"
Spirit of perfection,	"
Spirit of the elect children of God,	"
You, teacher and protector of the Church,	"
You, explorer of the human heart,	"
You, dispenser of heavenly graces,	"
You, counselor of the afflicted,	"
You, eternal light,	"

You, consuming fire,   "

You, fount of life,   "

You, spiritual union,   "

You, joy of angels,   "

You, illumination of the patriarchs,   "

You, inspiration of the prophets,   "

You, courage of the martyrs,   "

You, counsel of confessors,   "

You, purity of virgins,   "

You, beatitude of the saints,   "

Be merciful,   Protect us, O Lord!

Be merciful,   Graciously hear us, O Lord!

From every evil,   Deliver us, O Lord!

From the temptations of the enemy,   "

From the Spirit of deceit and lies,   "

From the Spirit of superstition,   "

From the Spirit of pride and envy,   "

From the Spirit of insult and injury,   "

From the Spirit of immorality,   "

From the Spirit of concupiscence and laziness,   "

From the Spirit of materialism and consumerism,   "

From the Spirit of opposition to the revealed truth,   "

From the Spirit of hardness of heart,   "

From eternal death,   "

We are sinners,   Hear our prayer!

Renew and sanctify all members of Your Church,   "

Guide and sustain Your Church,   "

Illuminate and sustain our Holy Father, the Pope,   "

Protect us from doctrinal error,   "

Reconcile all peoples and grant them Your peace,   "

Bring all nations to unity of faith in love,   "

Enflame the hearts of our young people

With the fire of Your love   "
Illuminate all peoples with Your divine inspirations,   "
Grant us the grace of perseverance,   "
Visit and deliver the souls in Purgatory,   "
Be our everlasting reward,   "
Lamb of God who takes away,
     The sins of the world,   Forgive us, O Lord!
Lamb of God who takes away
     The sins of the world, Graciously hear us, O Lord!
Lamb of God who takes away
     The sins of the world.   Have mercy on us!

- Send us Your Spirit! Alleluia!
- And You shall renew the face of the earth!
  Alleluia!

Let us pray:
O God, who by the light of the Holy Spirit illuminated the hearts of the faithful, grant that, in that same Spirit, we may be wise and ever rejoice in His consolation. Through Christ our Lord. Amen.

10) Blessing
Jesus, illuminate us with Your Spirit. Protect, heal, guide and transform us internally with the gifts of Your Spirit, show us Your truth and deliver us from eternal death. Jesus, You are the way, the truth and the life, and You live and reign with the Father in the unity of the Holy Spirit world without end. Amen.

JESUS, SEND US YOUR HOLY SPIRIT (II)

1) I adore You, Jesus, conceived by the Holy Spirit! I love You, Jesus, with the love of the Holy Spirit! I believe in You, through the work of the Holy Spirit.

2) Jesus, I adore You together with Mary, Your Mother, who conceived You by the Holy Spirit thereby becoming spouse of the Spirit. Thank You, Mary, for praying to Jesus together with me to fill me with His Holy Spirit.

- Jesus, I adore You with Mary, spouse of the Holy Spirit.

(Repeat this prayer quietly within yourself)

3) Jesus, full of the Holy Spirit, You worked for the good during Your earthly life. You did not do anything without the Spirit, who bonded You in love with the Father. You warned Your disciples not to leave themselves open to inspirations of the spirit of this world nor to the spirit of sin. That is why, Jesus, I am praying to You now to deliver me from the spirit of this world, which goes against the Spirit which acted in You, and which You promised to me:

- Free me from the Spirit of this world, so that it does not govern my heart!

(Repeat this invocation quietly within yourself)

4) Jesus, Your Spirit is a Spirit of humility, of openness to the Father's will and readiness to fulfill His wishes at any given time. In the world and in my heart,

You wish to drive away that spirit of pride which so easily takes root and governs us. That same spirit, which possessed the hearts of the first man and woman, governs in many hearts seducing them to go against the Father's will. Today, I renounce that spirit of pride and all its consequences in my life, in my relationship with others and with You. I want You to free me from that spirit of pride so that I can be possessed by Your Spirit which is open to the Father's will. I want to be possessed by that same Spirit to which Your Mother, Mary, opened Herself – a Spirit of Humility.

- Jesus, free me from the spirit of pride and all its evil seductions!

(Repeat this invocation quietly within yourself)

5) Jesus, the Spirit, which You promised to Your followers and which led You, is a Spirit of moderation in regard to material goods. You wished us to use these goods for our benefit and that of our fellow man and not that we become used by them and become enslaved by them. You know how easily I let myself be taken in by a spirit of greed and gluttony and I become blind to reason and intelligence, and to my heart. You know how easily my greed makes me mean and hard-hearted towards those who need my help. Today, in front of You, I renounce that spirit of greed and all its consequences in my life, in my relationship with others and towards You.

- Jesus, in Your name, I renounce the spirit of greed and I decide for generosity and merciful love!

(Repeat this prayer quietly within yourself)

6) Jesus, in You, purity ruled! You referred to all those of pure heart as 'blessed' because they would be able to see God. You know, Jesus, that also the spirit of impurity very easily overtakes me, my heart and my feelings become impure and I become incapable of seeing God. Today, I renounce the spirit of impurity and all that followed as a result of entertaining that spirit in my heart. In front of You, now, I renounce it. And with a clean heart, I accept myself, all those around me and the whole world, with that same Spirit of purity that You and Your Holy Mother inhaled an exhaled from Your profoundly pure souls.

- Jesus, in Your name, I renounce that spirit of impurity and immorality and I decide for the Spirit of Purity!

(Repeat this prayer quietly within yourself)

7) Jesus, in Your heart, You loved everyone and You did good to all. That is why You gave up Your life. You criticized those who had an envious eye and who could not feel joy over the well-being of others. Jesus, I too, have been envious of the successes of others and happy when things went badly for them. Today, in front of You, I renounce that spirit of envy and all its consequences in my relationships with others. Purify me completely of this so that a Spirit of simplicity and joy can take possession of my heart.

- Jesus, in Your name, I renounce the spirit of envy and jealousy and I decide for the Spirit of brotherly love and joy.

(Repeat this prayer quietly within yourself)

8) Jesus, during Your time here on earth, You ate and drank and feasted with Your friends. You used this image as a parable about the kingdom of God. To the hungry, You gave to eat and to the thirsty, to drink. You invite me to a Spirit of moderation. You know that the spirit of indulgence in food and in drink destroys me physically and spiritually. Today, in front of You, I renounce that spirit of gluttony and all its consequences in my life and its influence on my relationships with others and towards material goods. Deliver my heart so that I am not enslaved to food or drink, but that my spirit, supported by Your Spirit, can always be free.

- Jesus, deliver me from the spirit of gluttony and give me a Spirit of moderation.
  (*Repeat this invocation quietly within yourself*)

9) Jesus, You are meek and humble of heart. But You knew, too, how to show Your anger. When You found sacrilege in the temple in that it had become a marketplace, You took a rod, drove them out and overturned the money changers' tables. You said: "Be enraged, but do not let the sun go down on your anger!"

Jesus, I recognize that it is easy to make me angry, and that I lose control of my words and my behavior. Then I heavily offend You and those around me.

- Jesus, I renounce that spirit of anger and open my heart to Your Spirit of meekness and gentleness!
  (*Repeat this prayer quietly within yourself*)

10) Good Jesus! You worked and You called all those who work for You to do so while it is still daytime. In the parable, You praised the one who, with his given talents, worked until he received ten-fold, and You harshly criticized the lazy servant who buried his talents. Jesus, I recognize that I am easily contaminated by the spirit of laziness, that I do not decidedly collaborate with the Father's will, that I put off using my gifts and never develop them. Jesus, You wish to gather abundant fruit from my life because You poured abundant graces down upon me. Jesus, I renounce the spirit of laziness and every sluggishness in co-operating with the Father's will. I renounce also every consequence of the spirit of laziness in me and around me.

- Jesus, I renounce the spirit of laziness and I decide for hardworking collaboration with the Father's will in the world!

(Repeat this prayer quietly within yourself)

11) Blessing

Jesus, bless me, my family, my community, the Church and the whole world. Make us whole so that we can follow the invitation of Your Apostle Paul:

"Live by the Spirit, and you will no longer yield to self-indulgence. The desires of self-indulgence are always in opposition to the Spirit, and the desires of the Spirit are always in opposition to the desires of self-indulgence; they are opposites; one against the other; that is how you are prevented from doing the things that you want to. But when you are led by the Spirit you are not under the Law." (Gal 5:16-18)

Heal us from the ways of the flesh. The Apostle teaches us:

"They are sexual vice, impurity and sensuality, the worship of false gods and sorcery, antagonisms and rivalry, jealousy, bad temper and quarrels, disagreements, factions and malice, drunkenness, orgies and all such things. And about these, I tell you now, as I have told you in the past, that people who behave in these ways will not inherit the kingdom of God." (Gal 5:19b-22)

Jesus, heal us and fill us with the gifts of Your Spirit which the Apostle teaches us are:

"Love, joy, peace, patience, kindness, goodness, trustfulness, gentleness and self-control." (Gal 5:22)

Jesus, bless us and protect us and fill us with Your Spirit and His gifts. You who live and reign world without end. Amen.

I ADORE YOU WITH MARY,
FIRST OF THE NEW CREATION

(It is recommended that these prayers be prayed around the feast of the Immaculate Conception, December 8th)

1) Jesus, I adore You, because You renew the world! Jesus, I love You, You are the Savior of the world! Jesus, I believe in You, You are the Redeemer of the world!

2) Jesus, I adore You with Mary who, from her conception, was preserved from original sin and its consequences. You are the redeemer of the world. I glorify You and I praise You because the fruits of redemption were first seen in Her. I thank You, Jesus, because the soul of Your Mother, from the first instant of its existence, shone with the beauty of divine love. O, how beautiful, how magnificent were Her soul and Her heart because, from their beginning they were full of grace and, within Her heart and soul, the damaged relationship between God and man was restored. I bless You, Jesus, because Mary became the new dawn of that 'better day' which was due to come through Her with Your arrival. Thank You Jesus, because You found Yourself a worthy dwelling place.

- Jesus, I adore You together with Mary, conceived without sin!

(Repeat this prayer within yourself)

3) Jesus, I bless and I glorify You with Mary, because of Her sinless entry into this world. Her conception was foretold immediately after the first sin. In the book of Genesis it is written:

"Then Yahweh God said to the snake, "Because you have done this, accursed be you of all animals wild and tame! On your belly you will go and on dust you will feed as long as you live. I shall put enmity between you and the woman, and between your offspring and hers; it will bruise your head and you will strike its heel." (Gen 3:14-15)

O Jesus, that sinless woman foretold in Genesis is Mary, Your Mother, and You, Jesus are the fruit of Her womb who will crush and effectively destroy the head of Satan. She is the new Eve, the true Mother of the living, because spiritually She never experienced death nor was She tainted by sin.

- Jesus, I thank You and bless You with Mary, the Mother of the living.
  (Repeat this prayer quietly within yourself)

4) Jesus, while I am glorifying You, I am reminded of the moment of the glorious conception of Mary in the womb of Her mother Anna. Joachim and Anna had long awaited this event in prayer and fasting in this way preparing the dwelling place of the new and most beautiful and most pure creature Mary, who would – in turn – receive the most perfect gift to creation. I present the moment of Her conception to You now and I sing together with the Psalmist:

"Remember I was born guilty, a sinner from the moment of my conception. But You delight in sincerity of heart, and in secret

You teach me wisdom. Purify me with hyssop till I am clean, wash me till I am whiter than snow." (Ps 51: 5-8)

I thank You now with all my heart for the moment when, out of nothing, I became a living creature, when You called me into existence, when You gave me life. I thank You for that moment when Your creative love pronounced those words over me, 'let it be!' While I thank You for my life, I recognize also my fragility and I pray to You:

- Jesus, free me from sin and its consequences. Grant me, this very day, a new heart!
(Repeat this invocation quietly within yourself)

5) Jesus, while I remain before You thanking You for my life, I must consciously thank You for the love of my parents who cooperated with the Father's creative love. Reward them today for their love, Jesus. I know that they too have their faults; purify them. May they find joy in the new life that they created, working together with You. I wish that my love for my parents would be a fount of joy and peace for them. Forgive them their respective sins and heal them of the wounds which sin has caused. Heal the relationship between my mother and father. Heal also the wounds in my heart because of the imperfection of my parents and because what was lacking in their love caused deep wounds in my heart and my soul. By the power of Your love and the loving act of redemption, may love and gratitude for my parents be poured into my heart and into their hearts for me.

- Jesus, I adore You with the Immaculate Virgin for the parents which You gave to me!

103

(In silence, think about your parents, decide for love towards them, for forgiveness and reconciliation. If one or both of them have already passed away, pray for their eternal rest.)

6) Jesus, while I glorify Your act of redemption which manifested its fruitfulness in Mary, I bring before You all children who today are conceived in their mother's womb. May their parents rejoice in the gift of life and may they be welcomed in love! Protect them, Lord, from sin and everything which can darken or destroy the joy in their hearts. May every conceived child be protected from sickness and from the consequences of their parents' sin, and may they – even in the womb – rejoice in the gift of life! May all children be the fruit of love and cooperation with the Father's will. Grant, O Jesus, that not even one be the fruit of passion or lust or sin! May every mother feel joy at the conception of life, just as Anna rejoiced in the life of her daughter Mary!

  - Jesus, I adore You now in the name of all newly-conceived lives and in the name of their parents!

    (Repeat this prayer quietly within yourself)

7) Jesus, I know that it happens too that children are conceived who are neither wanted nor loved. Their parents do not rejoice in life, their mothers wish to take their lives. Many try to justify this but their reasons are often simply selfishness and the refusal to cooperate with the Father's will. He being the source of all life. Jesus, look now with special love on every mother who is experiencing the temptation to reject the life of her child. Grant that they meet up with someone who will give them

104

strength and help them to accept the gift of life with love. May the fathers of these newly-conceived children behave responsibly like Anna and Joachim at the knowledge of the existence of this new life.

- Jesus, I adore You and I decide for life in the name of all those who have decided for death.

(Repeat this prayer quietly within yourself)

8) Jesus, I now present You all those mothers who collaborate with the Father's will, who thankfully and joyfully accept the gift of life. May they be blessed, may their hearts be bathed in love and may all death be far away. May they find deep joy in their children! I present also all those who, seduced by sin, fear and anguish, and, not finding the necessary help, refuse the gift of life, and now suffer terribly and are in deep remorse. Heal them, Lord, and enable them to become apostles who use their negative experiences for positive ends. In doing reparation for their sin, may they be freed from any negative consequences and may they from now on live in joy and peace, accepting and serving life!

- Jesus, I praise You because Your mercy always triumphs and cancels every condemnation and delivers us into life!

(Repeat this prayer quietly within yourself)

9) Jesus, thank You because You came to serve life and You even gave Your life for us. I present to You now all doctors and hospital personnel, all women's counselors and advisors. May they always give the type of service worthy of the great gift of life. May respect for the unborn grow continually. Be blessed in all those who

consciously take care of new life with a deep sense of responsibility. Jesus, how easily we do away with life, how easily we advise for death! May Your Spirit of 'Life Giver' and 'Lover of Life' possess the hearts of those who help pregnant mothers so that they, too, like Mary in the womb of Her mother, find the conditions for development and growth. Grant that, from now on, no one serves death, but life and grant those, who want children and as yet have none, Your grace in reward for having joyfully yearned for life.

(In silence, continue to pray for doctors and those working in medicine)

10) Blessing

Jesus, bless us all her present, all people, all families, all pregnant mothers and all the unborn. Drive far from us the spirit of death and destruction. Enable us to serve life with love and deep respect. Through the intercession of Mary Immaculate, who conception we celebrate at this time, may the Spirit of life possess us, renew us, heal us and give us peace. You, who live and reign, world without end. Amen.

AND THE WORD BECAME FLESH

1) I adore You, Jesus, because You became man!
Jesus, I love You, because You so loved the world
that You came among us.
Jesus, I believe in You, because You renounced
Your heavenly glory to be with us.

2) Jesus, may that moment be blessed when, our of
all eternity in Your immense love, You decided to become
man, when You decided to leave the glory that You had
with Your Father in Heaven as the Only Begotten, when
You decided to become like us in all things – except sin.
Be blessed because, from eternity, You loved us with
immeasurable love. Be blessed and glorified, Jesus, for
having left Eternal Light, and entering the darkness of this
world in order to bring us into the light, which would
illuminate the way to eternal life. Be blessed for having
left Eternal Truth in order to be the Truth of this world.
May my heart sing to Your eternal wisdom by which You
freely decided to destroy the foolishness and pointlessness
of this world.

 - Jesus, I thank You and I glorify You for having
 decided to become man.
 (Repeat this prayer quietly within yourself)

3) Jesus, may You be blessed for all those prophetic
words which spoke of Your coming. Your coming was
the beginning of the new time, a better and more beautiful
time. That is why the prophet Isaiah sings, looking
forward to Your coming:

"Let the desert and the dry lands be glad, let the wasteland rejoice and bloom; like the asphodel, let it burst into flower, let it rejoice and sing for joy.

The glory of Lebanon is bestowed on it, the splendor of Carmel and Sharon; then they will see the glory of Yahweh, the splendor of our God.

Strengthen all weary hands, steady all trembling knees!

Say to the faint-hearted: Be strong! Do not be afraid. 'Here is your God, vengeance is coming, divine retribution; he is coming to save you.'

Then the eyes of the blind will be opened, the ears of the deaf unsealed, then the lame will leap like a deer, and the tongue of the dumb sing for joy; for water will gush in the desert and streams in the wastelands, the parched ground will become like a marsh and the thirsty land springs of water." (Is 35:1-7)

- Jesus, I rejoice in Your coming because You come to save us.

   (Repeat this prayer quietly within yourself)

4) Jesus, blessed be that moment when You chose Mary to be Your Mother, when already You had preserved Her from original sin and all other sin. Together with Her, I adore and praise You for the triumph of Her love in Her life. Mary, together with You, I praise that decision of Your Son, of which Isaiah prophesied:

"Listen now, house of David: are you not satisfied with trying human patience, that you should try the patience of my God too? The Lord will give you a sign anyhow: It is this: the young woman is with child and will give birth to a son whom She will call Immanuel." (Is 7:13-14)

I rejoice with you, Mary, because You are that virgin about whom the prophet spoke. You are virgin and mother. When, during Your childhood, You served in the temple as a virgin consecrated to the Lord, You fasted and prayed ardently, longing for the coming of the Messiah – the Emmanuel. You could not have even imagined that You would have been chosen one of the Lord.

- Jesus, I bless and praise You with Mary, the chosen Mother.

(Repeat this prayer quietly within yourself)

5) Blessed be that moment, Mary, when the angel Gabriel was sent to announce to You the joyful news of the near coming of the Messiah. Blessed be that moment, Mary, in which Your heart understood and welcomed the message of salvation:

"In the sixth month, the angel Gabriel was sent to a town in Galilee called Nazareth, to a virgin betrothed to a man named Joseph, of the House of Dave; and the virgin's name was Mary. He went in and said to Her: 'Rejoice, You who enjoy God's favor! The Lord is with You.' She was deeply disturbed by these words and asked Herself what this greeting could mean, but the angel said to Her: 'Mary, do not be afraid; You have won God's favor. Look! You are to conceive in Your womb and bear a son, and You must name him Jesus. He will be great and will be called Son of the Most High. The Lord God will Him the throne of His ancestor David; he will rule over the house of Jacob forever and His reign will have no end.' Mary said to the angel: 'But how can this come about since I have no knowledge of man?' The angel answered: 'The Holy Spirit will come upon You and the power of the Most High will cover You with its shadow. And so the child will be Holy and will be called Son of God. And I tell you this too: Your cousin Elizabeth also in

her old age, has conceived a son, and she whom people called barren, is now in her sixth month, for nothing is impossible to God.' Mary said: 'You see before you the Lord's servant, let it happen to me as you have said.'" (Lk 1:26-38)

> - Jesus, I adore You, together with Mary, and repeat Her words in my heart: "You see before You the Lord's servant."
> *(Repeat this prayer quietly within yourself)*

6) Jesus, all glory and praise be to that moment when You became man by the power of the Holy Spirit in the womb of the virgin Mary, and when Her heart became Your dwelling place. I adore Your mysterious Incarnation, the moment of your entry into this world. Mary, in Her humility and obedience, said, "Let it be" and You were able to come. With Your coming, a new way was open for God and mankind. That is why, You became 'Emmanuel – God with us,' letting God continue with man. You corrected the course of man's history with God, which from the time of the first sin had been plunged into darkness, mankind not wanting to face God anymore, hiding in fear, because it had not valued His friendship. Thank You, Jesus, that You are here with us. Together with the whole Church, I sing:

> *To God whom earth and sea and sky*
> *Adore and laud and magnify*
> *Whose might they own whose praise they tell,*
> *In Mary's body deigned to dwell.*

O, Mother blest, the chosen shrine
Wherein the architect divine,
Whose hand contains the earth and sky,
Vouchsafed in hidden guise to lie.

Blessed in the message Gabriel brought
Blessed in the work the Spirit wrought
Most blest to bring to human birth
The long desired of all the earth.

O Lord the virgin born, to thee
Eternal praise and glory be
Whom with the Father we adore
And Holy Ghost for evermore.

7) Jesus, Incarnate Word of God, blessed be that moment when Your Mother Mary left Nazareth to go to the hill-country to visit Your cousin Elizabeth. It was love which inspired Her and started Her on Her path to help Her cousin, who, in her old age, was expecting a child. Blessed be Her every step because She carried You, o Jesus, a living tabernacle, Your dwelling place.

Mary, blessed be the moment when Elizabeth blessed and thanked You because she recognized the Mother of her God. Blessed be the moment when, on meeting Your cousin, Your heart sang the Magnificat to God. In the womb of Elizabeth, the child leaped with joy, feeling the nearness of his deliverance from sin and its consequences.

I want my soul to unite with Yours now singing His praises, as You did:

111

My soul magnifies the Lord,
My spirit rejoices in God my Savior;
For he has looked with favor on his lowly servant,
And from this day all gernerations will call me blessed.
For He that is mighty has done great things for me,
*   And his body is His Name.*
He has mercy on those who fear Him in every
*   Generation.*
He has shown the strength of His arm,
He has scattered the proud in their conceit.
He has cast down the mighty form their thrones,
*   And has lifted up the lowly.*
He has filled the hungry with good things,
*   And has sent the rich away empty.*
He has come to the help of His servant Israel
*   For He has remembered His promise of mercy,*
*   The promise He made to our fathers*
*   To Abraham and his children forever*
(The Magnificat)

-   Jesus, like Mary, my soul magnifies the Lord
and my spirit rejoices because You are present
here!
        (Repeat this prayer quietly within yourself)

8) Jesus, I adore You because You are my God,
conceived in the womb of the Virgin Mary. You grew
beneath Her heart, just as all children develop within the
womb of their mother. Jesus, I know that, from the
moment of my Baptism, You also dwell within me and
that You reside in my heart. I want You to develop and

grow within me. I wish for my soul to be a fitting place for You. Therefore, purify me that I may worthily have You as my guest. Jesus, drive out whatever is hindering Your development within me, within my soul, with my heart and within my whole being, so that I become a living tabernacle of Your presence. I wish for my heart and my soul to be molded into Your likeness. Drive far from me all spiritual deformity and imperfection that I can be a spiritual 'incubator' and assume Your likeness.

- Jesus, make my life Your dwelling place!
    (*Repeat this invocation quietly within yourself*)

9) Jesus, I know that You are present in every baptized person, because he is immersed in Your death. Be blessed in all those who have put their hearts and souls at Your disposition so that you may develop and grow within them to fullness. Be blessed also in those who are wasting the grace of their Baptism or who have completely driven You out of their lives, because You are always capable of renewing Your graces within them, to dwell within them once more and be their God and for them to be Your people. I glorify You because You will heal them in soul and spirit and make their hearts free once again for You.

(*In silence, call to mind people you know and pray for them, people for whom you are responsible, who need your help, and those who, in some way, you may have led into sin.*)

10) Blessing
    Jesus, Incarnate Word in Mary's womb, I believe that You are present, and I beg You to speak Your word so that I can be healed in body and soul. Heal me so that

I can become a temple of Your presence, so that You may dwell within me. Heal the hearts and souls of all, of all families and communities. Bless Your Church so that it really becomes Your Body and a temple of your presence in the world. Bless and heal all sick people. May You, who remain with us by the power of Your Incarnation, be blessed and praised, glorified and honored now and forever because You live and reign world without end. Amen.

I ADORE YOU WITH MARY,
ASSUMED INTO HEAVEN

(These prayers are especially suitable for the Feast of the Assumption.)

1) Jesus, I adore You, because You are my God!
Jesus, I love You, because You bring to fulfillment all that You initiate!
Jesus, I believe in You, because You manifested Your glory in Mary!

2) Jesus, I adore You, because You are the glorified Lord. I thank You, because You sit at the right hand of the Father, interceding for us. I thank You, because, by the way You lived Your life, I recognize the way I must live mine. I bless You, because Your life becomes the reason for my hope and a foundation for my faith. I especially want to praise You today for Mary because, with the example of Her life, You show me the surest way to reach my heavenly home. Today, we celebrate Her Assumption into Heaven. You took Her – body and soul – into Heaven where You, together with the Father and the Holy Spirit, live and reign. May my heart sing, and completely open up to Your power and to Your love which was manifested in Her life.

- Jesus, I glorify You together with Mary, assumed into Heaven!

(Repeat this prayer quietly within yourself)

3) Lord Jesus, I wish to thank You today for the way Mary lived Her life. You had always been the center of Her life, Her reason for living. As a young girl, She prayed with a heart full of eager expectation for the coming of the Messiah. She had not the slightest intuition that She was the Chosen One who would be Your Mother. When, at the instant of the Annunciation, She became Your Mother, You were the center of Her existence. Everything She did, She did for You. That is why, together with the Church, I glorify You and sing:

My soul magnifies the Lord,
My spirit rejoices in God my Savior;
For he has looked with favor on his lowly servant,
And from this day all gernerations will call me blessed.
For He that is mighty has done great things for me,
*   And his body is His Name.*
He has mercy on those who fear Him in every
*   Generation.*
He has shown the strength of His arm,
He has scattered the proud in their conceit.
He has cast down the mighty form their thrones,
*   And has lifted up the lowly.*
He has filled the hungry with good things,
*   And has sent the rich away empty.*
He has come to the help of His servant Israel
*   For He has remembered His promise of mercy,*
*   The promise He made to our fathers*
*   To Abraham and his children forever*
(The Magnificat)

- Jesus, I glorify You because You glorified Your Mother!

(Repeat this prayer quietly within yourself)

4) Jesus, I know that everything worked out for the best in Mary's life because She loved You with all Her heart, all Her soul and all Her life. Thank You, Jesus, for having rewarded Her by taking Her body and soul into Heaven, for the faith which She had shown towards You from the time of conception. She gave birth to You in a rustic stable in Bethlehem, because no one welcomed Her – a pregnant woman – into his home. She warmed You with Her motherly love and, in Her own arms, She carried You into Egypt, protecting You from Herod who threatened Your life. Exile was not even difficult for Her or Joseph since it meant saving You.

- Jesus, I adore You and glorify You together with Mary, Your Mother, who protected You from Herod!

(Repeat this prayer quietly within yourself)

5) Jesus, Mary presented You in the temple and, even though it was a moment of deep happiness, She experienced anxiety and pain. The old man Simeon and the prophetess Anna were in the temple. Simeon rejoiced over the meeting, but he also foresaw the suffering, saying, even at that time, that you would be a sign of contradiction. St. Luke writes:

"Now in Jerusalem there was a man named Simeon. He was an upright and devout man; he looked forward to the restoration of Israel and the Holy Spirit rested on him. It had been revealed to him by the Holy Spirit that he would not see death until he had set

117

eyes on the Christ of the Lord. Prompted by the Spirit, he came to the temple; and when the parents had brought in the child Jesus to do for Him what the law required, he took Him into his arms and blessed God and he said: 'Now, Master, You are letting Your servant go in peace as you promised; for my eyes have seen the salvation which You have made ready in the sight of the nations, a light of revelation for the gentiles and glory for your people Israel.'"
(Lk 2:25-35)

- Jesus, I adore You in the temple with Your Mother who presented You there.
(Repeat this prayer quietly within yourself)

6) Jesus, I adore You, with Mary assumed into Heaven, because She educated You and taught You in Her motherly love. She brought You with them on pilgrimage to Jerusalem at the age of twelve. What pain She felt on realizing that She had lost You. I thank You, Jesus, that, on finding You among the doctors of the temple, Your words turned Her sorrow to joy. She kept Your words in Her heart and contemplated them often. She saw that the Father's will was of supreme importance in Your life, just as it had always been in hers, and it was because of His will that You had remained in the temple!

Thank you, Mary, because Your heart made a home for the Word of God – Your Son. Today, I wish for my heart to become like Yours that I may contemplate the love the Word of God.

- Jesus, may my heart watch over and contemplate Your words!
(Repeat this prayer quietly within yourself)

7) Jesus, I adore You and I thank You because, for a long time, You lived in silence and obscurity in Nazareth with Mary and Joseph, and, as Your Mother taught You, You grew in wisdom and knowledge before God and men. I bless You for every joy She experienced with You and every worry. Today, I thank You with Her because Her teaching was not in vain and is completely rewarded today.

Jesus, today I wish to become a member of that Holy Family of Nazareth – with You, Mary and Joseph. I wish to be obedient to You and to grow with You in wisdom and knowledge. I choose Mary today as my mother and teacher and I wish to be enrolled in Her school. I wish to go on the same path which You went with Her. I wish for all families to be like Your family, that all parents educate their children well and that all children grow in wisdom and knowledge before God and before men.

> \- Jesus, I adore You and I follow the example of You and Your Mother with all my heart and all my soul.
>
> (*Repeat this prayer quietly within yourself*)

8) Jesus, thank You because it was at Mary's request that You carried out Your first miracle. Thank You that She accompanied You on the road to Calvary, thank You that underneath the cross You gave Her to me as my mother and me to Her as Her child. She underwent everything together with You in Her heart and, together with You, She loved and forgave. And when death put an end to Your suffering, She continued to mourn and suffer for Your absence. Be blessed because it was to Her, first and foremost, that You came after Your Resurrection to

gladden Her heart. I thank You because She, together with the Apostles, prayed for the coming of the Holy Spirit and, with Her prayer and presence, She inspired the early Church. I thank You, Jesus, for Her whole life which She completely abandoned to Your service, and that She remained ever-faithful, humble and obedient. Thank You, Jesus, because in Her, we find a cause for our joy and hope, Mother of Perpetual Succor and Love.

Together with the prophet Isaiah, I rejoice because, in Her life, You created that which he had prophesied:

"I exult for joy in Yahweh, my soul rejoices in my God, for he has clothed me in garments of Salvation, he has wrapped me in a cloth of saving justice, like a bridegroom wearing his garland, like a bride adorned in her jewels." (Is 61:10)

9) Jesus, I bless You for that moment when Mary left this world to enter a better one, when She was assumed and glorified in Heaven, when what John describes in the book of Revelations was fulfilled in Her:

"Now a great sign appeared in Heaven: a woman, robed with the sun, standing on the moon, and on Her head a crown of twelve stars. She was pregnant, and in labor, crying aloud in the pangs of childbirth." (Rev 12:1-2)

Jesus, may my heart recognize in Her the strength of Your Spirit, the path my life should take and the end I should arrive at. May my heart sing, together with all the angels and saints, and never cease to rejoice because You uplift the lowly. May my soul be adorned with the virtues with which Her soul was adorned so that, I too, one day can share in the beatitude of the saints.

-   Jesus, I magnify Your name because You raise the lowly and prepare glory in Heaven for them!
    (Repeat this prayer quietly within yourself)

10) Blessing

Jesus, I pray to You together with Mary, assumed and glorified in Heaven, to bless me with all the blessings in Heaven and on earth. Heal me in body and soul that I may be freed from all fear of death. Bless my family, my community and the whole world. By Her intercession, may I be delivered from all evil and all its seductions. Fill our hearts and souls with the strength of the Spirit in which your Mother breathed and served up until Her earthly end, You who live and reign world without end. Amen.

JESUS, I ADORE YOU, TOGETHER WITH THE QUEEN OF PEACE

1) Jesus, I adore You because You are the King of Peace!
   Jesus, I adore You because You are the source of peace!
   Jesus, I believed in You because You are our peace!

2) Jesus, I adore You today, together with the Queen of Peace, whom You sent to be with us during these restless times. May that moment be forever blessed when, She said to the visionaries:

"I am the Queen of Peace. My Son sends me to help you."

May You be blessed through Her because, in Your name, She continually invites us to open ourselves up to peace.

"Dear children! Today, I thank you and I want to invite you all to God's peace. I want each one of you to experience in your heart that peace which God gives. I want to bless you all today. I am blessing you with God's blessing and I beseech you, dear children, to follow and to live my way. I love you, dear children, and that is why I have been calling you – I do not know how many times – and thank you for all that you are doing for my intentions. I beg you, help me to present you to God, to save you and to lead you on the way of salvation. Thank you for having responded to my call."

(June 25, 1987-6th Anniversary of the apparitions)

- Jesus, I adore You, together with the Queen of Peace, and I open my heart to peace!
  (Repeat this prayer quietly within yourself)

3) Jesus, King of Peace, I adore You, together with the Queen of Peace. Blessed be that moment when She appeared at the big cross crying, saying:

"Peace, peace, peace! Only peace! Peace between God and man, and peace between all people! Fast and pray, because with fasting and prayer, even wars can be stopped!"

Thank You for sending the Queen of Peace, to show us that peace comes from You and to make clear to us under what conditions peace will come. These conditions are conversion and reconciliation through prayer and fasting. Thank You, Jesus, for letting Her sow the seeds of peace in these turbulent times. I thank You and bless You, together with all those who have opened their hearts to Her motherly call and who have received the gift of peace, because they prayed and fasted, and because they confessed and participated in the Holy Mass.

- Jesus, I adore You, together with the Queen of Peace and all those who opened their hearts to the invitation to peace.
  (Repeat this prayer quietly within yourself)

4) Jesus, I adore You, together with the Queen of Peace who, in Your name, invites me and teaches me peace in my heart. She gives me the strength to be a witness to that peace in my family and in my everyday life situations. In her message, She said:

"Dear children! I call you to peace. Live peace in your heart and all around you, so that all will know the peace that does not come from you but from God. Little children, today is a great day. Rejoice with me! Celebrate the Nativity of Jesus with my peace. It is for this peace that I have come as your Mother, the Queen of Peace. Today I give you my special blessing. Bring it to all creation, so it will know peace. Thank you for having responded to my call." (December 25, 1988)

(Think about yourself, your family and neighbors and pray for peace and serenity in your relationships.)

5) I adore You, Jesus, together with the Queen of Peace, who teaches me that hatred is dangerous, that it gives birth to division and discord and that It leads the soul to restlessness and lack of peace. The Queen of Peace warns us that Satan is very strong and very active:

"Dear children! Hatred gives birth to dissension and does not see anyone or anything. I call you always to bring harmony and peace. Especially, dear children, in the place where you live, act with love. Let your only instrument always be love. By love, turn everything into good that Satan wishes to destroy and to possess. Only that way, shall you be completely mine and I shall be able to help you. Thank you for having responded to my call." (July 31, 1986)

My Jesus, today I wish, with all my heart, to do what Mary says in Your name. I renounce hatred and all that creates disorder and lack of peace in me and around me. I renounce Satan and all his wicked works. I

124

renounce all types of cooperation with Satan. In Your mercy and through Her intercession, I will resist every temptation.

(Think about what threatens peace within you, within your family, in your circle of friends and acquaintances and decide for peace, renouncing all cooperation with dissension, division and evil.)

6) Jesus, I adore You and I thank You, together with the Queen of Peace, who makes it possible to contribute to peace in the world with my prayer and sacrifice, my love and peace. Jesus, You wish to make me an apostle and a witness of peace in the world. How many people today have no peace? How many young people are agitated to the point of destructiveness? How many families are disunited? How much heartbreak is there? How many nations are in conflict with others?!

Thank you that I can help Mary in Her battle against evil and against the deception of Satan:

"Dear children! By your own peace, I am calling you to help others to see and begin to seek peace. You, dear children, are at peace and not able to comprehend lack of peace. Therefore, I am calling you to help destroy everything that is evil in people, by your prayer and your life, and to uncover the deception that Satan makes use of. Pray that the truth prevails in all hearts. Thank you for having responded to my call." (September 25, 1986)

- Jesus, together with You and Mary, I wish to bring peace and love, to expose and conquer Satan and his plans in the world!

(Repeat this prayer quietly within yourself)

7) Jesus, I adore You and glorify You, together with Mary, the Queen of Peace, and all those who, upon Her invitation, have opened their hearts to Her messages, putting into practice all Her maternal advice, experiencing Your mercy and forgiveness at confession. May You be blessed, Jesus, for Your mercy, because You have pulled many hearts out of the grip of sin and have entered into many destructive lifestyles, opening the way to peace. Be blessed in all those who, by the intercession of Mary, have understood that they have to love their lives as well as the lives of others without condition, thereby opening a new way to peace.

Be blessed, Jesus, for every priest who patiently and responsibly hears confessions and, with great love, opens hearts to Your peace and forgiveness. Be blessed because, by Mary's intercession, you will rescue and open many other hearts which are now closed.

(Call to mind and pray for those who you know are in need of confession that they may be able to recognize their own sinfulness and be granted the strength to come forward to be delivered.)

8) Jesus, I adore You and I acknowledge that I did not heed Your words which came through Your Mother Mary. The seed of divine peace, which She was sowing, fell on the untilled land of many hearts, therefore, war came and all that war brings with it. That is why nations could not understand or agree with one another. And now, before You, I want to repent for the sin of war and for all the destruction and killing. I want to repent for the extent to which I ignored Your messages, thereby, contributing to the lack of peace. We did not recognize

the time of our 'visitation.' Many lives were taken, the spirit of violence and hatred became stronger than the blessed Spirit of Peace in most hearts.

Many joined forces against Your Mother's messages, doing all in their power to stop or silence them. I am sorry, Jesus, that hearts became so hardened and cold. Jesus, evil continues to threaten but, I believe that it is possible for You to turn all to good and that, there where sin di most abound, Your grace will abound even more.

> -   Jesus, I adore You, together with Mary, the Queen of Peace, and I beseech You, forgive us our sins of war and all destruction of human life!
> *(Repeat this prayer quietly within yourself)*

9) Jesus, I adore You and I thank You for the hope that You give to me through Mary, the Queen of Peace, during these troubled times. I know that conversion is the path that must be followed before peace comes, but often neither I nor those around me have the strength to walk it. That is where I need to call upon Your grace. I thank You, Jesus, that today You will give me the strength to convert and to understand the ways and the laws of peace. May no person tire on his road of conversion that will bring him to peace. St. James contemplates and invites us:

"Where do these wars and battles between yourselves first start? Is it not precisely in the desires fighting inside your own selves? You want something and you lack it; so you kill. You have an ambition which you cannot satisfy; so you fight to get your way by force. It is because you do not pray that you do not

receive; when you do pray and do not receive, it is because you prayed wrongly, wanting to indulge your passions." (Jas 4:1-3)

Purify me and this whole world, Jesus, with the grace of conversion, so that my deepest yearning may find its fulfillment in You, and so that I may be delivered from disordinate passions which, in turn, are a threat to peace. Enable Your Church to be an instrument of blessing with peace! I know, Jesus, that, for my part, I need to be open and willing in order for Your Spirit to possess and deliver me. Thank You, Jesus, for granting inner freedom and peace to those who invoke Your help.

(Think about and pray for those who do not cooperate with the Lord or accept His Mother's messages or the gift of Her presence.)

10) Blessing

Jesus, King of Peace, by the intercession of Mary, grant us Your peace. May it rule every heart and soul, every family and community and finally, the Church and the whole world. Heal all aggression and division, heal every wound received from a family or community without peace. Heal also the wounds inflicted by the restless of the Church or from the world. Touch every restless heart by the intercession of the Queen of Peace. Renew the Church and the world and grant that, by the intercession of the Queen of Peace, justice and peace may be embraced through You, who live and reign, world without end. Amen.

JESUS, I ADORE YOU, TOGETHER WITH
ALL YOUR SAINTS (I)

1) I adore You, Jesus, fount of life and holiness!
I love You, Jesus, love of all the saints!
I believe in You, Jesus, hope of all who are saved!

2) Jesus, today I wish to adore You, together with the whole of the heavens and the earth, with the Church glorified in Heaven, the Church suffering in Purgatory, and the Church militant on earth. You are the head of the Church, the High Priest, because You gave Your life for all of us. You are the glory of all the glorified and all who await glory. You are the love of all those immersed in immeasurable love in Heaven, and the love of all who yearn for the unending love. To You, I wish to sing now, together with the whole Church:

For all the saints who from their labors rest,
Who Thee by faith before the world confessed
Thy name, O Jesus, be forever blessed.
Alleluia, alleluia!

Thou wast their rock their fortress and their might;
Thou, Lord, their captain in the well-fought fight;
Thou in the darkness drear their one true light.
Alleluia, alleluia!

O, may thy soldiers faithful true and bold,
Fight as the saints who nobly fought of old,
And win with them, the victor's crown of gold.
Alleluia, alleluia!

O, blest Communion! Fellowship divine!
We feebly struggle, they in glory shine;
Yet all are one in Thee, for all are Thine.
Alleluia, alleluia!

And when the strife is fierce, the warfare long,
Steals on the ear the distant triumph-song,
And hearts are brave again, and arms are strong.
Alleluia, alleluia!

The golden evening brightens in the west;
Soon, soon to faithful, warriors cometh rest;
Sweet is the calm of paradise the blest.
Alleluia, alleluia!

But lo, there breaks a yet more glorious day;
The saints triumphant rise in bright array;
The king of glory passes on his way.
Alleluia, alleluia!

From earth's wide bounds, from oceans' farthest coast,
Through gates of pearl streams in the countless host,
Singing to the Father, Son and Holy Ghost.
Alleluia, alleluia!

> - Jesus, High Priest, head of the Church, I adore You together with the whole Church!
> *(Repeat this prayer quietly within yourself)*

3) Jesus, I adore You and thank You today that You invite me also to unity with You, together with all the saints. I want to awaken today an awareness of the unity

between all the members of Your Church and rejoice with all of them. I wish for my heart to continually rejoice in You because You have called me to the order of the redeemed who, in their weakness, experienced Your strength. I want to be part of that beatific vision which St. John beheld:

"In my vision, I heard the sound of an immense number of angels gathered around the throne and the living creatures and the elders; there were ten thousand times ten thousand of them and thousands upon thousands, loudly chanting:

Worthy is the Lamb that was sacrificed
To receive power, riches, wisdom,
Strength, honor, glory and blessing.

Then I heard all the living things in creation,
Everything that lives in Heaven and on earth,
And in the sea crying:

To the one seated on the throne
And to the Lamb,
Be all praise, honor, glory and power,
Forever and ever."
(Rev 5:11-13)

\-   Jesus, I adore You and I sing: "All power and honor, glory and praise be to the Lamb forever and ever."
    (Repeat this prayer quietly within yourself)

4)   Jesus, I adore You, together with Mary, the Mother of the Church, the Mother of all Saints, the Queen of Heaven and Earth, of all Prophets and Martyrs, of all the saved.   To Her, first and foremost, You gave Your grace to participate in Your holiness, to be Your Mother and to reign with You.

Mary, thank You, because I know that You are my mother and today, in the company of all the saints, I decide for You.   Thank You that, in Your messages, You teach me that I can be holy, despite all my trials and my natural inclination to sin and despite all the traps that Satan wishes to lay before me.   You say to me:

"Dear children! I beseech you to take up the way of holiness beginning today. I love you and, therefore, I want you to be holy. I do not want Satan to block you on that way. Dear children, pray and accept all God is offering you on a way, which is bitter. At the same time, God reveals all sweetness to whoever begins to go on that way, and he will gladly answer every call of God. Do not attribute importance to petty things. Long for Heaven. Thank You for having responded to my call." (July 25, 1987)

Mary, rejoicing and glorifying today with You and with all the saints who have reached eternal beatitude, I decide for holiness.   I recognize my own weakness, my sinfulness, the attachment I have to myself and to this world.   I am aware of the alluring ways and the deceptions of the evil one, and that the road to virtue is even bitter at times.   But I know, too, that You are one step ahead of me with Your help all the time and, therefore, I respond with my whole heart and my whole soul:

- Jesus, I adore You and, together with Mary and all the saints, I decide to take the road of holiness!

(Repeat this prayer quietly within yourself)

5) Jesus, I adore You because You are first among martyrs. You gave Your life for us on the cross. I adore You, together with all those who followed You along that path and who, with their whole lives, were ready to suffer for You, loving their enemies. I glorify You, together with all the martyrs of all times who gave their lives for You, nailed to a cross, or thrown before wild animals in the arenas, killed by imprisonment, concentration camps or by the enemy's sword. I adore You, together with all the martyrs of my own nation. They now sing in joyful praise to You. May I feel the reverberations of their praises in my heart. Your power manifested itself in their weaknesses. I adore You now for all those who have no fear in witnessing for You because they know that, even if their earthly lives are taken, anew and more wonderful and eternal life awaits them, and that the price of this gift is to live and carry one's cross, to love and to forgive. I bless you because You accepted their pain, their suffering, their tears and their distress and turned it into the seed of Christianity for others. I adore You, Jesus, because You give meaning and purpose and You reward those who remain faithful to the end with a halo of victory and glory. Jesus, how I desire that, today in the place of my weakness, Your strength could be glorified.

- Jesus, I adore You and glorify You with Mary, the Queen of Martyrs, and with all Your martyrs!

(Remember the martyrs of your own nation and thank and praise God for their example and their strength)

6) Jesus, I adore You, with all those in Heaven who, having persevered in works of mercy and love, have reached heavenly glory. I adore You with all those who now, at Your invitation, do as You instructed when You said:

"So, always treat others as you would have them treat you: That is the law and the prophets." (Mt 7:12)

I adore You, together with all those who secured themselves a place in the house of the Father, because they followed Your instructions which St. Matthew writes about in his Gospel:

"Do not store up treasures for yourselves on earth, where moth and woodworm destroy them and thieves can break in and steal. But store up treasures for yourselves in Heaven, where neither moth nor woodworm destroys them and thieves cannot break in and steal. For wherever your treasure is, there will be your heart also." (Mt 6:19-21)

Jesus, today I decide to store up that blessedness which does not wear away or decay, with which You have already rewarded my brothers and sisters who now delight in adoring You in Heaven. Purify my heart and soul of all greed and selfishness, so that I may find the way out of my small-mindedness and enter that big-heartedness which enriched the lives of those who followed You. Be blessed in all those who recognized Your image in their brothers. Be blessed and praised in those who imitated You with love just as You invited us to do.

- Jesus, I adore You, together with all those who, doing acts of mercy, arrived at their heavenly home!

(Repeat this prayer quietly within yourself)

7) Jesus, toady I adore You, together with all those who lived Your Word and brought it to others. I adore You, together with all the holy popes and bishops, religious communities and missionaries and all holy mothers and fathers who, by the way they lived, brought the good news to others. Be praised because You walked with them, and by the power of Your Spirit, they became Your witnesses and lived Your Word. Be praised for all those who reached Heaven because of their obedience to Your Word. I adore You, Jesus, together with all those unknown to me who, in silence and suffering, sometimes even in sickness, earned their heavenly reward and now glorify You continuously. May the Pope, the bishops, priests, religious orders and all Your people, all Your Church journeying through the trials of this life, decide for holiness, listening to and fulfilling Your Holy Word. May those who announce Your Holy Gospel live long and fruitful lives. Look down in Your mercy on those who feel that their suffering is in vain because too much of Your Word falls on arid ground. May an awareness of their unity with You and with all the saints, encourage and inspire them.

(In silence, think about your parish priest and priests and nuns you know, about your bishop and parents, and pray for them.)

8) Jesus, I adore You, together with all the Saints of Heaven, who endlessly rejoice before Your face. During their lives, You gave them the grace to know You as being good and merciful. They knew You as the One who accepts sinners and forgives them. I thank You for all those who, after a life of sin, welcomed Your mercy and returned to the Father's house with all those who loved

135

much, because they had been forgiven much. I praise You because You are the hope of sinners who now journey through this life and of those who reject You and who do not respond to Your love. You seek them out and forgive them. I praise You, Jesus, for those who are now enslaved to the powers of evil because You will deliver them and guide them to their heavenly home of love and peace for eternity.

(Pray now for all those you know who live far from Jesus' love. Pray that they may be led into the Community of Saints.)

9) Jesus, I adore You and I sing Your glory, together with all the Angels and Archangels and with the whole heavenly court. I want to readily respond to the invitation of the prophet Isaiah:

"Be joyful and glad forever at what I am creating, for look, I am creating Jerusalem to be 'joy.'

I shall be joyful in Jerusalem and I shall rejoice in my people. No more will the sound of weeping be heard there, nor the sound of a shriek." (Is 65:18-19)

- Jesus, I adore You and sing to You:
  Holy, holy, holy Lord
  God of power and might
  Heaven and earth are full of Your glory!

  (Repeat this prayer quietly within yourself)

10) Blessing

Jesus, You crown and glory of all the saints, by the intercession of Mary and the saints, bless me, protect and deliver me from evil. Put me on the road to peace and holiness. Heal me in body and soul, turn all things to good. Bless my family, the Church and the world. Comfort and encourage all those who suffer, illuminate those in darkness, convert those in sin, seek the lost so that the heavens are full of those giving thanks. Grant that none lose their way. Together may we sing Your glory, You who, together with the Father in the Holy Spirit, live and reign world without end. Amen.

JESUS, I ADORE YOU, TOGETHER WITH
ALL YOUR SAINTS (II)

1) Jesus, I adore You because You are the Most High!
Jesus, I love you because You are most worthy!
Jesus, I believe in You because You invite us to holiness!

2) Jesus, I adore You and I beseech You to send Your Spirit that sanctifies me. I wish to listen to and fulfill Your Word. I want to go through life with it treasured in my heart because Your Word is holy. I wish to travel this world, meet people, work and live with them in Your Spirit that sanctifies, guides, and illuminates.

- Jesus, send me Your Holy Spirit to guide my footsteps!

(Repeat this invocation quietly within yourself)

3) Jesus, I adore You and I wish to be poor in spirit while I adore You, always free from any attachment to material goods. In my heart, I wish to find only You. I adore You with all the saints because they managed to remain detached, poor in spirit, and so I praise You now. I adore You for all those whom You will free from temptations, created by wealth and material goods, and who will decide for the road of holiness.

- Jesus, You said: "Blessed are the poor in spirit for theirs is the Kingdom of Heaven!"

(Repeat this prayer quietly within yourself)

4) Jesus, I adore You, together with all those who, in this valley of tears, have discovered true joy. I adore You with those who are now afflicted, who feel alone, hurt, humiliated or mistreated, because You do not forget them. I adore You in the name of all those who seek fulfillment in the abuse of drugs, alcohol, immoral behavior and in the search for power. I adore You in the name of all those who, with their behavior, cause heartbreak to others, because You will help them to see Your light.

- "Blessed are those who suffer, because they shall be consoled!"

(Repeat this prayer quietly within yourself)

5) Jesus, I adore You, together with all those whose meekness won them their heavenly reward. I bless You because You will make my heart meek and humble too and deliver me from all pride and feelings of superiority! I adore You in the name of all those who suffer at the hands of the proud, the violent and the overbearing because, meditating Your meekness, they will find the strength to remain on the narrow road to sanctity. I adore You, together with all those who have been left without their fatherland, their homes or without food. You will not forget them, O Jesus. You can find a way to touch the hearts of the rich and the powerful and inspire them to share.

- "Blessed are the meek for they shall inherit the earth!"

(Repeat this prayer quietly within yourself)

6)   Jesus, I adore You, together with all the just and the upright in Heaven, because they sing to Your justice. I bless You, Jesus, because You have put a hunger and thirst for justice in the heart of every man. I praise You for all those who have decided to live and work according to Your justice.

I present to You the bitterness of all those who have suffered injustices. Grant that they do not fell forced to harden their hearts. Instead, may they rejoice in Your Spirit, believing Your Word!

-       "Blessed are those who hunger and thirst for justice, because they shall be satisfied!"
(Repeat this prayer quietly within yourself)

7)   Jesus, I adore You, together with all the Saints in Heaven, because it was Your mercy which saved them. I rejoice in Your mercy which forgives and sanctifies. I adore You, together with all those who have decided for mercy and renounced ruthlessness and cruelty, because, in that way, we have on earth witnesses to Your mercy. I adore You in the name of all those who inspire and communicate violence and cruelty, who have no mercy for themselves or for those around them in their families, in their communities and in the world, because Your mercy will touch them and transform them.

-       "Blessed are the merciful for they shall be shown mercy."
(Repeat this prayer quietly within yourself)

8)   Jesus, I adore You with Mary, who was pure of heart. In Her, there was no trace of sin. Her heart was pure because there was never any attachment to Herself or

to the world, and so She could always look at God. I adore You, Jesus, together with all the Saints who, in their walk through life, cleansed their hearts from sin with the help of Your grace, and managed to maintain a purity of heart and detachment from earthly and worldly goods. Passion never dominated them and they were always able to see God in every situation. They now enjoy the beatific vision in its fullness.

Jesus, I open my heart to You. You know that it is not pure and so neither are my eyes, my words and my behavior towards myself or others. While I adore You, I beseech You to cleanse me, to purify me, so that I may see You and, through You, my heavenly Father. I present to You now all those whose hearts are not pure and who, therefore, have become blind. They cannot see You nor those around them, and with their unclean hearts, they soil and pollute the lives of those around them. Purify us, O Lord!

- "Blessed are the pure in heart for they shall see God!"

(Repeat these words of Scripture quietly within yourself)

9) Jesus, I adore You, together with all the saints, whose hearts rest in Heaven and enjoy the peace of eternal life. I praise You for all those who are living in the world today and are working for peace. They are peacemakers because they forgive and love, because they are merciful and gentle of heart.

Jesus, our hearts are often caught up in a spirit of hatred and unrest, a spirit of cruelty and revenge, and so we become incapable of receiving peace and much less of being peacemakers. Many unborn children never make it to life because a merciless hand reaches them before they have even come into the world. O Jesus, pour the Spirit of Peace into our hearts – and conflict and war will be no more.

- "Be blessed in all those who forgive, thereby creating peace! Blessed are the peacemakers for they shall be called sons of God!"
(Repeat this prayer quietly within yourself)

10) Jesus, I adore You because You said that those who are persecuted in the cause of justice are blessed and will inherit the Kingdom of Heaven. Be blessed in all the Saints who suffered without desiring revenge, without a spirit of violence. Like You, they were able to suffer persecution in the cause of right, maintaining their peace and their well-wishing towards all. Look down today on all the persecuted, on those who are mistreated and who suffer because they are different, because they think differently or practice different faiths, or have a different nationality. Look down on those who are persecuted by those nearest to them, by their families who are left alone, hurt and humiliated. May all their suffering lead them along the road of faith and hope in love. And, when we suffer, help us realize, Jesus, that it is always better to suffer as the 'sinned against' than as the 'sinner!'

- "Blessed are you when you are persecuted in the cause of right, because yours is the Kingdom of Heaven!"
(Repeat this prayer quietly within yourself)

11) Blessing

Jesus, in the Beatitudes, You outlined the values of the Kingdom of God. Bless us and heal us so that we may accept and live Your Word. Free us from all evil, purify our hearts, make them merciful, peacemaking, hungry for justice and poor in spirit; make them like Your own heart. Heal the sick, deliver those enslaved by sin, and may the restless find peace in You, who with the Father and the Holy Spirit live and reign world without end. Amen.

JESUS, NEWBORN KING, I ADORE YOU

1) Jesus, I adore You, newborn Word of God!
   Jesus, I love You, Emmanuel – God with us – in
   the form of a newborn child!
   Jesus I believe in You, my newborn King!

2) Jesus, I adore You, together with Mary, who gave
birth to You in the stable in Bethlehem, because, in the
hearts of men, there was no place for You. I adore You
because You chose to be born poor and humble. I adore
You just as Mary and Joseph adored You then. Jesus, my
newborn King, I wish to glorify You just as Mary invites
me to:

*"Dear children! Today in a special way, I
bring the little Jesus to you, that He may bless you
with His blessing of peace and love. Dear children,
do not forget that this is a grace, which many people
do not comprehend and accept. Therefore, give all of
yourselves, you who have said that you are mine, and
seek my help. First, give your love and example in
your families. You say that Christmas is a family
feast, therefore, dear children, put God in the first
place in your families, so that He may give you peace
and protect you not only from war, but also in peace,
from every satanic attack. When God is with you, you
have everything. But when you do not want Him,
then you are miserable and lost, and you do not know
on whose side you are. Therefore, dear children,
decide for God. Then you will receive everything.
Thank you for having responded to my call."*
(December 25, 1991)

- Jesus, here I am before Your manger. I give You my heart. From now on, I decide for You!
  (*Repeat this prayer quietly within yourself*)

3) Jesus, I adore You with Mary, Joseph and all the angels who, on that holy night, came in their choirs singing songs of joy. Singing, they announced Your coming and Your plan. You came to teach us to glorify God in the highest and, in that way, became people of goodwill. I bless, glorify and adore You and I sing.

May my soul vibrate with joy, may my heart out of love sing together with all the Courts of Angels:
- "Glory to God in the highest and peace to His people on earth!"
  (*In silence, repeat this prayer.*)

4) Jesus, I adore You, together with all those who tonight are singing Your praises. Be blessed and praised because You come among us as a little baby, whose presence inspires joy and opens hearts to peace. Be blessed in those who com as shepherds with gifts which show the important place you have in their hearts so that all hearts can learn from them to put You in the first place. Be blessed for all those, who, like the shepherds, after having adored You, have the courage to witness to Your love. St. Luke writes for us:

"Now it happened that when the angels had gone from them into Heaven, the shepherds said to one another: 'Let us go to Bethlehem and see this event which the Lord has made known to us.' So they hurried and found Mary and Joseph, and the baby lying in a manger. When they saw the child, they repeated what had been told about Him, and everyone who heard it was astonished at what the

145

shepherds had said to them. As for Mary, She treasured all these things and pondered them in Her heart. And the shepherds went back glorifying and praising God for all they had heard and seen, just as they had been told." (Lk 2:15-20)

- Jesus, I adore You and I glorify You with Mary and Joseph, the angels and the shepherds!
   (Repeat this prayer quietly within yourself)

5) Jesus, on that holy night, also all of nature bowed down before You. The Kings of the east noticed and followed a new star. With fatigue and difficulty, they persevered until they found You in Bethlehem and they gave You gifts worthy of a King. Jesus, I bless You and I adore You, together with the Kings, in the name of all those who are searching. Grant, O good Jesus, that they find You.

Before Your manger, I wish to experience the same joy as those kings in my heart when they beheld Your blessed little face. Open my eyes, Jesus, that I may recognize the signs in my life which lead to You. In Jerusalem, the learned who knew the Scriptures presided, but their hearts were closed and their eyes blinded, and they could not recognize Your coming. I adore You in the name of all those who know all about You but do not recognize You as their God and Savior. I sing to You, together with the whole Church:

1) Adeste fideles;
   Laeti triumphantes;
   Venite, venite in Bethlehem;
   Natum videte regem angelorum:

Venite adoremus (2)
Venite adoremus Dominum.

O Come all ye faithful,
Joyful and triumphant,
O come ye, o come ye to Bethlehem;
Come and adore him, born the king of Angels:

> *O come let us adore him (2)*
> *O come let us adore him, Christ the Lord.*

2) *Deum de Deo,*
   Lumen de lumine,
   Gestant puellae viscera:
   Deum verum, genitum non factum:
   > *God of God,*
   > *Light of lights*
   > *Lo! He abhors not the virgins womb;*
   > *Very god, begotten not created:*

3) *Cantet nunc lo!*
   Chorus angelorum:
   Cantet nunc aula celestium;
   Gloria in excelsis Deo!

> *Sing choirs of angels,*
> *Sing in exultation,*
> *Sing all ye citizens of Heaven above:*
> *Glory to God in the Highest!*

4) *Ergo qui natus*
   Die hodierna
   Jesu tibi sit Gloria:
   Patris aeterni Verbum caro factum!

   Yea Lord! We greet thee,
   Born this happy morning,
   Jesus, to thee be glory given
   Word of the father, now in flesh appearing!

(Think about and pray for those who, locked in their own refusal to believe and in their self-security, have not bothered to look for Jesus – not even at Christmas.)

6) Jesus, I adore You in the name of those who fear You like Herod and, therefore, decide to kill You. Mary, blessed be that moment when, together with Joseph, You escaped into Egypt saving the life of Your Son. I adore You, Jesus, in all those who, with their sins, their evil words and deeds and their evil behavior, have either killed You or hindered Your growth in themselves or in those around them. I praise You, Jesus, because You will unite them to You. You will open their hearts and they will live in peace and free from fear, helping others to discover Your peace. Jesus, I adore You in the name of all those who have become violent towards themselves and others, especially towards children and young people. Many of them have tragic ends because they are not aware of their heavenly Mother who will protect them. Grant, Jesus, that, this Christmas, they experience protection and security. May they feel today also how You have come to bring peace and joy.

(Call to mind and pray for those who have lost their way because of disorder in their family)

7) Jesus, I adore and thank You because, with Your coming, You have established a unity between God and mankind and between man and his fellow man. Be blessed in all those who will reconcile for Christmas, who will forgive and decide for love. Be blessed in those who will feel a call to help the sick and the disabled. Jesus, many are left alone and forgotten by others and, for them, Christmas is a sad and difficult time.

- Jesus, I present them now to You; be with them, and open up new possibilities for company and love.
(Present to the Lord the lonely and the sick you know and decide that, for Christmas, you will bring them comfort, peace and help, or that you will do some act of love.)

8) Jesus, I adore You today. You are my God and Lord, the Messiah and Savior. Thank You, because You are with me as a little baby who inspires love. I present to You now all the children of the world, those who have a family and those who are abandoned, those who suffer because of broken marriages and those who suffer because of drunkenness in their families and those who will not feel the joy of Christmas, because they are sick or in pain. May the heart of every adult today be directed to children in an effort to comfort their pain, and may joy return again and shine on children's faces.

- Jesus, may Your coming awaken joy and happiness in the hearts of children and their parents so that peace may reign in every family!
(Repeat this prayer quietly within yourself)

9) Jesus, I adore You on this day of peace. May peace descend on this world, immersed in division, conflict and war. May every heart today welcome peace, may all guns be silent and all conflicts halt because You came to this world to bring peace. May every heart, every family, every community, every nation and the whole world today embrace justice and peace.

(Think about the conflicts in the world and present by name the powerful people of the Church and the world, and pray in your own words for peace.)

10) Blessing

Jesus, You are with me today as a little infant. Bless me and heal my soul. Fill me with peace and goodwill so that I may participate in Your project of peace. Calm the restless and protect the insecure. Be a friend to the lonely. Bless our families, our communities and the Church, so that the Spirit of Christmas, the Spirit of Peace and Joy, may reign in the world through You who, with the Father and the Holy Spirit, live and reign world without end. Amen.

JESUS, I ADORE YOU AT THE BEGINNING
OF THIS NEW YEAR

1) I adore You, Jesus, because You are the Eternal Word of God.
   I love You, Jesus, because You are the beginning of a new era!
   I believe in You, Jesus, because my time is in Your hands!

2) I adore You, Jesus, together with Mary, who is with You now in eternity, because She was with You in everything She did during Her time on earth. Everything She did was for You. You had always been the very purpose of Her life on earth. You were the fulfillment of Her time, the beginning and end of every moment, every hour, every day, every year of Her whole life. In Her message, She says to us:

"Dear children! I call you to prayer, so that you will encounter God in prayer. God gives Himself to you. But He wants you to answer to His call in full freedom. That is why, little children, set aside a time during the day to pray in peace and humility and to meet God, the Creator. I am with you and I intercede for you before God. So, watch in vigil, so that every encounter in prayer be a joyful meeting with God. Thank you for having responded to my call."
(November 25, 1988)

Mary, I want to be with You now before Jesus at the end of this year. I want to finish it in thanksgiving for the time past and begin the new year with You and Jesus. I thank You because I know that You, Mother, are with

151

me at this moment. I know that You will intercede for me and that I will have a joyful encounter with the Father and the Son and the Holy Spirit.

- Jesus, I adore You with Mary at the end of this year and at the beginning of the coming one.
(Repeat this prayer quietly within yourself)

3) Jesus, I adore You because You existed from eternity with the Father and the Holy Spirit. All time belongs to You, because You are God from God, Light from Light, true God from true God. You are the Alpha and the Omega, the beginning and the end. I adore You and I thank You because, in Your eternal love, You show me that I, too, exist together with You before the creation of the world and, in the same love. You ensure me eternal life. And, while I contemplate the passing of time, I want to become aware of what St. Paul teaches me, O Jesus:

"Blessed be the God, the Father of our Lord Jesus Christ, who has blessed us with all the spiritual blessings of Heaven in Christ. Thus He chose us in Christ before the world was made to be holy and faultless before Him in love, marking us out for Himself beforehand, to be adopted children, through Jesus Christ. Such was His purpose and good pleasure, to the praise of the glory of His grace, His free gift to us in the Beloved, in whom, through His blood, we gain our freedom, the forgiveness of our sins." (Eph 1:3-7)

- Jesus, be forever blessed, together with the Father and the Holy Spirit, because You chose me for Yourself before the existence of creation.
(Repeat this prayer quietly within yourself)

4) Jesus, I adore You because, through You, the Father grants me the grace of spending time here on earth – days, months, years. Be blessed because my time is immersed in Your infinite time, O Jesus, and You are present in my time every day. I thank You for my birth into time, as we know it, and for my baptism which plunged me into eternal time, freed from original sin. I thank You because time, as I know it, will one day meet up with and spill into Your eternal time, just as now the past is meeting with the future, the old year passes into a new. I wish to thank You now for all the days of my life and, in a special way, for the days of this year now drawing to a close. Be blessed because Your love accompanies me, because You are Emmanuel – God with us – every day, every moment. During this time, make me conscious of the swiftness of the passing of time and its irretrievable condition – we cannot turn back the clock! Every moment is unique, every moment is offered to me in Your love to grow in that same love. Thank You for every moment when I was conscious of this and I joyfully and thankfully cooperated with You. Forgive me those times that I wasted or used baldly, when I thought only of myself, using my time for my own selfish ends. I now put it into Your hands and pray with the Psalmist:

"In You Yahweh I take refuge, I shall never be put to shame.
In Your saving justice rescue me, deliver me, listen to me
And save me.
Be a sheltering rock for me, always accessible; You have
Determined to save me, for You are my rock, my fortress.
My God, rescue me from the clutches of the wicked, from
The grasp of the rogue and the ruthless.
For You are my hope, Lord, my trust Yahweh since childhood.

On You I have relied since my birth, since my mother's womb,
You have been my portion, the constant theme of my praise.
Many were bewildered at me, but You are my sure refuge.
My mouth is full of Your praises, filled with Your splendor all the
Day long.
Do not reject me in my old age, nor desert me when my strength
Is failing...
Prolong my old age and comfort me again.
For my part, I will thank You on the lyre for Your constancy,
My God.
I will play the harp in Your honor, Holy One of Israel.
My lips sing for joy as I play to You, because You have redeemed
Me, and all day long my tongue muses on Your saving
Justice..."

(Ps 71:1-9 and 21-24a)

    -   In You, Jesus, my soul sings and rejoices,
because You have saved me!

(Repeat this prayer quietly within yourself)

5) I adore You, Jesus, and I thank You, because You are my strength, my signpost, my life, my joy and my whole journey. I know that, without You, I can do nothing. I now put into Your hands and good that I have achieved. Purify my good acts if they are tainted with selfishness, with erroneous intentions, with the shadow of egoism, with pride, with a desire to show myself self-sufficient, and forgive me for those times when I took all the merit and the glory, robbing what really belongs to You.

I thank You for all the good in my family, in the community, in the Church, in my country and in my people. Grant that this evening thanksgiving rises from every heart. May peace-filled hearts sing to You. Grant that none of Your graces remain hidden and unappreciated.

(*Contemplate all the good you managed to do and offer thanksgiving to God for it.*)

6) I adore You, Jesus and, this evening, I recognize and admit that I am guilty of wrongdoing, and, that many times, I gave evil a free reign and it accumulated within me. It left its scars and bad will. I know that I often collaborated with evil and that my heart was often possessed by mistrust, anger and aggression. Often a spirit of revenge, pride and envy prevailed. I bring it all before You this evening and abandon it all to Your mercy. I want to walk together with You in this new time, completely purified, freed and unburdened. Heal my will so that I may joyfully walk closer to You. Jesus, I want to listen and fulfill what Your Mother tells me:

"Dear children! Today, I want to wrap you all in my mantle and lead you all along the way of conversion. Dear children, I beseech you, surrender to the Lord your entire past, all the evil that has accumulated in your hearts. I want each one of you to be happy but, in sin, nobody can be happy. Therefore, dear children, pray and, in prayer, you shall realize a new way of joy. Joy will manifest itself in your hearts and thus you shall be joyful witnesses of what I and My Son want from each of you. I am blessing you. Thank you for having responded to my call." (February 25, 1987)

155

- Jesus, I adore You and I give You now my past, my present and my future so that, unburdened, I may walk with You, my God, Emmanuel!

(Present everything that was negative to the Lord, repent it and make new resolutions.)

7) Jesus, I adore You at the end of the old and the beginning of this new year. I want to be of the same mind as Mary at the moment of Your incarnation when She said, "I am the servant of the Lord, may it be done unto me according to His will." I now wish to accept joyfully all that he Father and You, in Your love, wish to give me. I wish that my cooperation be total, without reserve and without resistance to the Father's will. I accept with a heart full of thanks the gift of time which You are giving me, O Jesus, and I pledge my complete willingness. I believe that, also for me just as I am, you have a plan for my life. Your Mother tells me:

"Dear children! Behold, also today, I want to call you to start living a new life as of today. Dear children, I want you to comprehend that God has chosen each one of you, in order to use you in His great plan for the salvation of mankind. You are not able to comprehend how great your role is in God's design. Therefore, dear children, pray so that, in prayer, you may be able to comprehend God's plan with you. I am with you so that you may be able to bring it about in all its fullness. Thank you for having responded to my call." (January 25, 1987)

- Jesus, I adore You and I believe that You have a place for me in Your plans. May Your will be done!
  (Repeat this prayer quietly within yourself)

8) Jesus, I adore You with all those who adore and love You because You are the Master of Heaven and earth. I thank You, together with all others who appreciate Your goodness, and I praise You, together with all who praise. I want my heart to unite with theirs so that, together, we may sing Your praises.

I adore You in the name of all those who do not adore You and who do not know You. I love You in the name of those who do not love You or have had no experience of Your love, those who hate You and speak evil of You. I believe in You, Jesus, in the name of all those who do not believe, or who have chosen to believe in false gods, who have given themselves to empty beliefs, refusing the truth.

I accept You, Jesus, my King of Peace, in the name of those who do not want You or Your peace, who prefer violence and conflict and let themselves be led by a spirit of evil.

- Jesus, Lord of Time, may this be a new beginning for me and for all peoples and nations!
  (Repeat this prayer quietly within yourself)

9) Jesus, I adore You and I present to You all those who began the new year this time last year, but are no longer among the living. You have called them into Your kingdom. I present to You all the victims of war and violence, all those who died in road accidents and in

various disasters, who died suddenly and unprepared. Be merciful with them, O Jesus! I present those who died in intense suffering, especially the young victims of drugs, alcohol and AIDS.

(Remember those who have passed away and pray for their salvation.)

10) Jesus, I present to You all those who, during this year, will cease to exist in this world. Grant that their leaving will be a passing into Your Kingdom. May they hear Your voice and my they respond in peace. Grant that no-one meets You unprepared or is taken by surprise. May we all keep vigil and awake in cheerful expectation. Grant that I and all others are waiting just as You, Jesus, say in the Gospel of St. Matthew:

"Who, then, is the wise and trustworthy servant whom the master placed over his household to give them their food at the proper time? Blessed that servant if his master's arrival finds him doing exactly that. In truth I tell you, he will put him in charge of everything he owns. But, if the servant is dishonest and says to himself: My master is taking his time', and sets about beating his fellow servants and eating and drinking with drunkards, his master will on a day which he does not expect and at an hour he does not know. The master will cut him off and sent him to the same fate as the hypocrites, where they will be weeping and grinding of teeth." (Mt 24:45-51)

(Reflect and pray now on the moment of your death and place it into the hands of the Lord. Offer to Him also the people who will be near you at the moment of your death, and pray also for those dying or agonizing as they die a slow death now.)

158

11) Blessing

Father, I beseech You in the name of Your Son, Our Lord Jesus Christ, in the Holy Spirit, to show me Your face, to have mercy on me. Take me by the hand and guide me through time and space. Heal me and enable me to remain faithful. Bless my family, the Church, my people and all people and nations. Drive from us all evil and give the strength to combat evil and to have the victory over it so that we, too, may enter into Your kingdom where You reign together with the Father and the Holy Spirit forever and ever. Amen.

(The following are texts that may be suitable for meditating at this time)

"Dear children! Also today, I am inviting you to a complete surrender to God. Dear children, you are not conscious of how much God loves you. That is why, He permits me to be with you to teach you and help you to find the way of peace. This way, however, you cannot discover if you do not pray. Therefore, dear children, forsake everything and consecrate your time to God, and God will bestow gifts upon you and bless you. Little children, do not forget that your life is fleeting lie a spring flower, which today is wondrously beautiful but tomorrow has vanished. Therefore, pray in such a way that your prayer and your surrender to God may become like a road sign. That way, your witness will not have value for yourselves but for all eternity. Thank you for having responded to my call."

(Message of March 25, 1988)

"Dear children! I invite you to open yourselves to God. See, little children, how nature is opening itself and is giving life and fruits. In the same way, I invite you to live with God and to surrender completely to Him. Little children, I am with you and I want to introduce you continuously to the joy of life. I desire that everyone may discover the joy and love which can be found only in God and which only God can give. God does not want anything from you but your surrender. Therefore, little children, decide seriously for God because everything else passes away. Only God does not pass away. Pray to be able to discover the greatness and joy of life that God gives you. Thank you for having responded to my call."
(Message of May 25, 1989)

***

"Bless Yahweh my soul, from the depths of my being,
Holy His name; bless Yahweh my soul, never
Forget His acts of kindness.
He forgives all of your offenses, cures all your diseases.
He redeems your life from the abyss; crowns you with
Faithful love and tenderness;
He contents you with good things all your life, renews
Your youth like an eagle's.
Yahweh acts with uprightness, with justice to all who are
Oppressed; he revealed to Moses His ways, His great
Deeds to the children of Israel.
Yahweh is tenderness and pity, slow to anger and rich in faithful
Love.
His indignation does not last forever nor His resentment remain
For all time; He does not treat us as our sins deserve,
Or repay us as befits our offenses.
As the height of Heaven above us, so strong is His faithful
Love for those who fear Him.
As the distance from east to west, so far from us does
He put our faults.
As tenderly as a father treats His children, so Yahweh treats
Those who fear Him.
He knows of what we are made, He remembers that we are dust.
As for human person, his days are like grass, he blooms like the
Wild flowers; as soon as the wind blows, he is gone, never
To be seen there again.
But Yahweh's faithful love for those who fear Him is from eternity
And forever; and His saving justice to their children's
Children; as long as they keep His covenant, and carefully
Obey his precepts."
(Ps 103:1-18)

JESUS, I ADORE YOU, SEND WORKERS
INTO YOUR HARVEST

1) I adore You, Jesus, because the Father sent You to save us.
   I love You, Jesus, because You love every person immensely!
   I believe in You, Jesus, because You were the first to reap the Father's harvest!

2) Jesus, I adore You, together with Your Mother, because She was Your first co-worker in the salvation of humanity because She, just like You, gave Her whole life for all people. She was able to do this because She followed You closely with prayer and sacrifice.

Thank you Mary, for Your collaboration with Your Son Jesus, because You have become the co-redemptrix of humanity, the Mother of our High Priest, the Mother of the Apostles and of all who work for the salvation of mankind. You are the Mother of all priests, the Mother of the whole Church, the Mother of all who preach the Good News. Thank you, Mary, because the Father found You ready and worthy to entrust You with the plan of salvation. Thank You because You desire that I, too, become open and willing to do the will of God – just like You. In Your message, You say to me:

"Dear children! Also today I give thanks to the Lord for all that He is doing for me, especially for this gift that I am able to be with you also today. Dear children, these are the days in which the Father grants special graces to all who open their hearts. I bless you and I desire that you too, dear children,

162

comprehend the graces, and place everything at God's disposal so that He may be glorified through you. My heart carefully follows each one of your steps. Thank you for having responded to my call."
(December 25, 1986)

    -    Jesus, I adore You, together with Mary, and I put myself at Your disposition for the realization of Your plans.

    (Repeat this prayer quietly within yourself)

3) Jesus, I adore You with the Father in the Holy Spirit, who called the prophets to announce the Good News, to invite to conversion, to strengthen, lead and ward people and nations. I praise You, together with all those who accepted Your invitation and who participated in the plan of salvation. Jesus, together with them, I want to accept Your invitation too. Like Jeremiah, I know that I am weak and unworthy, but I wish to collaborate. In the Book of Jeremiah it is written:

"The word of Yahweh came to me saying: Before I formed you in the womb, I knew you; before you came to birth, I consecrated you; I appointed you as a prophet to the nations. I then said: Lord Yahweh, you see, I do not know how to speak: I am only a child! But Yahweh replied: Do not say: I am only a child, for you must go to all to whom I send you and say whatever I command you. Do not be afraid of confronting them, for I am with you to rescue you. Yahweh declares. Then Yahweh stretched out His hand and touched my mouth, and Yahweh said to me: There! I have put my words into your mouth. Look, today I have set you over the nations and kingdoms, to uproot and to know down, to destroy and to overthrow, to build and to plant...

As for you, prepare yourself for action, stand up and tell them all I command you. Have no fear of them and in their presence I will make you fearless." (Jer 1:4-10,17)

Jesus, raise up prophets in Your Church and send them to Your people. May they accept, respond and fulfill their mission. Grant that they may be faithful to You. Today I say to You:

> - Jesus, here I am! With Your Spirit, send me, accompany me and all others who have responded to Your call.
>
>   *(Repeat this prayer quietly within yourself)*

4) Jesus, I adore You and I thank You that You prayed to the Father to send workers into the harvest and that You invited us to pray in the same way. In this way, You showed Your love to all those who needed to hear the Good News announced. St. Matthew writes:

> *"Jesus made a tour through all the towns and villages, teaching in their synagogues, proclaiming the good news of the kingdom and curing all kinds of diseases and illnesses. And when He saw the crowds, He felt sorry for them because they were harassed and dejected, like sheep without a shepherd. Then He said to His disciples: "The harvest is rich but the laborers are few, so ask the Lord of the harvest to send out laborers to His harvest."*
> (Mt 9:35-38)

The Father is the master of the harvest and the harvest is the People of God to whom the Good News should be announced. Lord Jesus, together with You, I pray to the Father to call young people, to give them the strength to respond with generosity to Your call and to work with dedication for the spreading and growth of

Your reign. Bless all parents, teachers and all in the profession of education and annunciation that they may become witnesses of Your Good News. Father, I beseech You, together with Jesus, the first worker in Your harvest, to send workers to the harvest.

(In silence, meditate on your family, your community and on yourself and pray to become an announcer of the Good News.)

5) Jesus, I adore You and I thank You for choosing educating and sending the first disciples on the mission of announcing the Good News. St. Matthew writes:

"After this, He summoned the twelve disciples and gave them authority over unclean spirits with power to drive them out and to cure all kinds of diseases and illnesses." (Mt 10:1)

Jesus, be blessed in all priests, bishops and the Pope whom You send on the same mission today. May they fulfill their calling in the strength of the Spirit. May they announce the Good News, drive out evil spirits and heal illnesses. May the strength of Your Spirit accompany them, and may signs and wonders follow them so that the world may see that they really are Yours.

Look down on those who are tired, disillusioned and alone. Grant that, through their suffering, they abandon themselves and rest in You. Be blessed in all those who suffer for You; grant that their suffering transforms itself into joy.

(Now remember and present to the Lord the priest who baptized you, the bishop who confirmed you, and all catechists and parish priests, deacons and religious brothers and sisters.)

6) Jesus, I adore You and I thank You, for the moment when You called Your first disciples to follow You. St. Matthew tells us:

"As He was walking by the Lake of Galilee, He saw two brothers, Simon, who was called Peter, and his brother Andrew,; they, were making a cast into the lake with their net, for they were fishermen. And He said to them: 'Come after me and I will make you fishers of people.'" (Mt 4:18-19)

Today, Jesus, pass by our families, our schools, on our streets and the places where the young meet, and invite them to be fishers of people. Grant that they respond joyfully and with dedication to their mission. Grant that the Spirit accompanies them on their way.

- Jesus, call the young and help them to respond generously to Your call!

(Repeat this invocation quietly within yourself)

7) Jesus, I adore You and thank You for those who are already on the road to the priesthood, because You have called them. Be blessed in every heart that has responded and wishes to follow You seriously. Be blessed in all the seminaries and novitiates and in all the places where people are educated to answer Your call. May those who respond grow in love of You and their neighbor and may love grow also towards the path to which they are called. You know all their problems, Lord, look after them. May they grow in the true faith and remain faithful to Your Word. May those who guide and educate them be full of that same love as You had for Your disciples. I adore You, Jesus. I beg You to protect them during their studies so that their faith may not be harmed, but become stronger and better and may they worthily serve their

people. May their educators guide them towards You and help to deliver them of every fear of You and of life itself. *(Reflect on and pray for those who you know are thinking about or have started out on religious life)*

8) Jesus, I adore You and I thank You for having sent Your Apostles to the end of the earth and having promised to be with them always and that You would accompany their words with signs and miracles. Be blessed in all missionaries who have responded to Your call and are now bringing Your Word to the ends of the earth. You know every one of them because it was You who called them. May each one now feel that You are near Him and that You will never abandon Him. You know too, Lord, all those who are in trials now, who are persecuted, mistreated, or who live in poverty in order to be with those to whom You sent them. Continue to invite young souls. Grant them the grace to respond generously so that all the ends of the earth hear and accept Your Word. Jesus, convert all those who evangelize in the name of false faiths, unify all Christian missionaries so that they can announce You in love and unity. You are the One True God and there is no salvation under other names. *(Reflect on and pray for those who have already answered the call of missionary and for new missionaries.)*

9) Jesus, I adore You because You are that tireless disciple and You constantly sacrifice Yourself for us. You know, Lord, that many joyfully answered Your call but have become tired, without motivation and without joy in their lives. Many of them have left their vocations and

returned to the world. You know also those who have strayed, profaned their calling and have shocked your people. Jesus, You can help them, You can heal them, You can bring peace and joy back to them and make them once again into witnesses of Your love in the world. I now pray for them.

(Reflect on and pray for those who you know are having difficulties in their vocations, and especially for those who have left.)

10) Blessing

Jesus, You are the real "fisher of men" because, with Your love, You heal us all, deliver us all, render us capable and call us. May Your blessing now descend on all priests and religious, our bishops and the Pope. Grant that they may serve the mysteries of faith joyfully. May Your blessing descend on all, may it lend peace and drive away all obstacles on their road through life. May Your love give strength to the youth, that they may answer the call; grant that families educate and render their children capable to embrace religious vocations. You who are our High Priest, the Good Shepherd, who lives and reigns, together with the Father in the Holy Spirit forever and ever. Amen.

JESUS, I COME TO ADORE YOU
SO THAT LOVE CAN BE LOVED

1) Jesus, I adore You, because You are eternal and immeasurable love!
Jesus, I love You, because You loved me first with an eternal love!
Jesus, I believe in You, because Your love inspired You to be present here with me.

2) Jesus, I come to You and I want to be with You, I want to return Your love. I desire that, from now on, Your love is loved within me. I do not come before You alone because I know that my love is so miserable that it can hardly respond to the depths of Your unconditional and immeasurable love. I come with Mary, Your Mother, who loved You with every fiber of Her heart and soul, body and mind.

Thank You, Mary, that I can spend this time and that, with Your love, You will make up for what is lacking in mine. My heart and my soul are neither prepared nor worthy to encounter Jesus, but I wish to meet Him. I thank You, Mary, that You have said to me in Your message:

"Dear children! From day to day, I wish to clothe you in holiness, goodness, obedience and God's love, so that from day to day, you become more beautiful and more prepared for your Master. Dear children, listen to and live my messages. I wish to guide you. Thank you for having responded to my call." (October 24, 1985)

- Jesus, clothe me in holiness, goodness, obedience, and love so that I, together with Mary, may return Your love!
  (*Repeat this invocation quietly within yourself*)

3) Jesus, I adore You and I want Your love to be loved in all churches and chapels where You dwell in the Eucharistic bread. You remained with Your people to protect them with Your love. Be blessed in all those who respond to Your love and try with all their hearts to love You as You deserve. I want to unite now with them and sing to You now in my soul.

Jesus, I know that in many churches and oratories You are abandoned and that Your people have forgotten You. It is there that I desire to return Your love, in the name of those who remain cold to Your love and deaf to Your invitations. Help them and give them the grace to understand the depth, the width and the beauty of Your love. May it possess them – body and soul. May it free them from evil and open them to Your love.

- Jesus, I adore You here and in all Your churches all over the world, and I desire that Your love be loved.
  (*Repeat this prayer quietly within yourself*)

4) Jesus, I adore You and I desire that Your love be loved where it is not appreciated, where it is humiliated, where it is trampled upon and offended. I know my beloved Jesus, that Your Eucharistic love is profaned in the occult, in black masses and in satanic sects, and that You suffer, are trampled on and despised there. Today I offer You my love in reparation for the offenses against

170

Your Eucharistic love. I wish to deeply respect, adore and love You in every profaned host, in every heart which is in sin and without love for You. I love You in those who make communion with You cold heartedly, who receive You without a thought.

> - Jesus, I adore You and love You wherever You are profaned and despised!
> *(Repeat this prayer quietly within yourself)*

5) Jesus, I adore You and I desire that Your love is loved in every human heart. I know, Jesus, that there, where human life is taken, aborted or not appreciated, they are rejecting Your love! That is why I want to love especially those who are in danger of losing their opportunity to live because their parents have decided to abort. I want to love You in the unborn life where the mother does not feel any joy because of the problems it will cause, or because she knows that the father of the child will now abandon Her.

Jesus, You laid down Your life with love for every life conceived and for the salvation of all. I praise and thank You, my Jesus, because you have identified Yourself with every person, as St. Matthew explains:

"Then the upright will say to him in reply: 'Lord, when did we see You hungry and feed You, or thirsty and give You drink? When did we see You a stranger and make You welcome, lacking clothes and clothe You? When did we find You sick or in prison and go to see You?' And the King will answer: 'In truth, I tell You, in so far as You did this to the least of my brothers, you did it to me.'" (Mt 25:37-40)

- Jesus, I adore You and love You in all the forsaken!

(Repeat this prayer quietly within yourself)

6) Jesus, I adore You and I desire that your love be loved in families. Be blessed in all those families, where both husband and wife consciously live in love for one another, thereby consolidating the strength of Your love. Be blessed in all those families, where Your love prevails between parents and children, the elderly and the young, the sick and the healthy. I know, Jesus, that in many families love does not reign, even though You love them and You give Your life for them. You wish to enrich them with Your love, to unify and to give peace but they do not accept Your love, they scorn it and refuse it.

Jesus, today I desire with all my heart and soul that Your love becomes something precious in every family, that it becomes a foundation and inspiration of conjugal and reciprocal love and of all personal relationships within the family. May all members of every family be touched by Your immense love and, in that way, be enabled to love one another and respond to Your love.

(Present your family to Jesus, mention every member by name and present other families that are having problems. Do not judge them, instead pray for them.)

7) Jesus, I adore You, and I wish to love Your love in all the Christian Churches which have become so divided, who judge and refuse each other so much that they have become scandalous for the whole world. Your desire was that those who believe in You should become one, just as You are in the Father and the Father is in You:

"This is my commandment: love one another, as I have loved you. No one can have greater love than to lay down his life for his friends. You are my friend if you do what I command you. I shall no longer call you servants because a servant does not know the master's business; I call you friends, because I have made known to you everything I have learnt from my Father. You did not choose me, no, I chose you; and I commissioned you to go out and to bear fruit, fruit that will last; so that the Father will give you anything that you ask Him in my name. my command to you is to love one another." (Jn 1:12-17)

> - Jesus, with You, I pray to the Father. Grant that Your love be loved in all Christian communities!
> *(Repeat this prayer quietly within yourself)*

8) Jesus, I adore You, and I desire that Your immense love be loved in every creature and in all of creation because Your love does not exclude anyone or anything; it embraces the whole of creation. I admit, Jesus, that it is difficult for me to understand how You can love even those who hate You, who refuse and despise You. You love the just and the unjust, the evil and the good. Your love is not a reward for goodness; it is the cause of every good, the inspiration to true love, and that is why You do not exclude anyone. Lord, You know me. You know my limits and how limited my love is, and how difficult it is for me to love those who do not love me. I am still a long way from that love which manages to embrace all, excluding nobody. Now, praying before You on my knees, I wish my love to become all-inclusive. Forgive me, Jesus, that I have excluded so many of Your

beloved children form my love. I was closed and locked form inside. I could not even receive that love which You were transmitting. But now, You have made me realize that I cannot refuse to love those whom You so ardently love.

(Reflect on and pray for the gift of love for the persons who do not love you or whom you do not love.)

9) Jesus, I adore You and I thank You for Your immeasurable love. It is Your will that I, too, love in this way but You know how limited my love has become. For this reason, I renounce all that hinders the growth of Your love within me and that keeps my love so miserable. I renounce all the contamination of my past life. I wish to renounce also in the name of those who do not wish to renounce, and who continue to act in an unloving way.

(Present to Jesus now all the negative experiences of the past and decide to pray every day for the gift to love.)

10) Blessing

Jesus, I believe in the strength of Your love, with which You love me and every other creature without any cause or boundary. Heal my heart and soul, fill me with Your love. Fill with Your healing love all families, all communities, our Church and all Christian Churches, all those who belong to different faiths. Fill with Your healing love all those who despise and scorn You, all those who are possessed by hatred and sin, all those who are sick in spirit soul and body.

May Your love descend upon us, may it heal us, may it heal all division and make us happy. May that same love that pours out from Your heart towards the Father in Holy Spirit, now flow out from every heart towards all men and towards You who lives and reigns, world without end. Amen.

JESUS, IT IS WONDERFUL FOR US
TO BE HERE

1) Jesus, I adore You, because You prayed on Tabor!
Jesus, I love You because You showed Your glory
to the Apostles!
Jesus, I believe in You because of You, the Father
said: "This is my beloved Son!"

2) Jesus, You are hidden from my eyes, but I adore
You with Mary who, in Her motherly heart, always had a
foresight of the splendor of Your face and of the sublimity
and the glory which You possessed right from the
beginning. I adore You, with the Apostles Peter, James
and John, to whom You gave the grace to see the glory of
Your face and to hear the Father's voice. Blessed be that
moment when a deep yearning to remain on Tabor
emerged in Peter's heart. He wanted to stay there, not
because Tabor and the other mountains were so beautiful,
but because of the beauty and sublimity of Your face. I
wish to be with You now, Jesus, just as the Apostles were
with You on Tabor. Jesus, I desire to pray, to listen, to
reflect and to meditate. I also want to contemplate the
beauty of Your face and feel that strong desire for You
and for Your presence.

Forgive me that my eyes are often blind and my
ears have often not heard You, and that I often have not
seen or yearned for You. I now feel that yearning:
- Jesus, enable my heart and soul to feel always
the joy of Your presence!
(Repeat this invocation quietly within yourself)

176

3) Jesus, I adore You, and I beg You to send Your Holy Spirit to me so that I can deeply understand and live what happened during the transfiguration, as it is written by St. Luke:

"Now about eight days after this had been said, He took with Him Peter, John and James, and went up the mountain to pray. And it happened that, as He was praying, the aspect of His face was changed and His clothing became sparkling white. And suddenly, there were two men talking to Him; they were Moses and Elijah appearing in glory and they were speaking of His passing which He was to accomplish in Jerusalem. Peter and his companions were heavy with sleep, but they woke up and saw His glory and the two men standing with Him. As these were leaving, Peter said to Jesus: 'Master it is wonderful for us to be here; so let us make three shelters, one for You, one for Moses and one for Elijah.' He did not know what he was saying. As he was saying this, a cloud came and covered them with its shadow; and when they went into the cloud, the disciples were afraid. And a voice came from the cloud saying: 'This is my Son, the chosen One, listen to Him.' And after the voice had spoken, Jesus was found alone. The disciples kept silence, and at that time, told no-one what they had seen." (LK 9:28-36)

Thank You, Jesus, that You prayed on Tabor and thank You for having shown the disciples the sublimity of Your being. I repeat the Father's words before You. May my love and decision for You grow and develop throughout my life.

- This is my Son, the Chosen One, listen to Him!

(Repeat this prayer quietly within yourself)

4) Jesus, I adore You. You are the chosen One of my heart and my life. My soul now sings inspired by the words of the Psalmist:

"How lovely are Your dwelling places, Yahweh Sabaoth.
My whole being yearns and pines for Yahweh's courts.
My heart and my body cry out for joy to the living God.
Even the sparrow has found a home, the swallow a place
> *To nest its young – Your altars Yahweh Sabaoth,*
> *My King and my God.*
How blessed are those who live in Your house, they shall praise You
> *continually.*
Blessed those who find their strength in You, whose hearts are set on
> *Pilgrimage.*
As they pass through the valley of Balsam, they make there a water
> *Hole, and a further blessing, early rain fills it.*
They make their way from height to height, God shows Himself to
> *Them in Zion.*
Yahweh, God Sabaoth, hear my prayer, listen, God of Jacob.
God, our shield, look and see the face of Your anointed.
Better on day in Your courts than a thousand at my own devices,
> *To stand on the threshold of God's house than to live in the*
> *tents of the wicked.*
For Yahweh God is a rampart and a shield, He gives grace and
> *glory; Yahweh refuses nothing good to those whose lives are*
> *blameless.*
Yahweh Sabaoth, blessed is he who trusts in You.

- Jesus, may my heart and my sould yearn for You!

(*Repeat this prayer quietly within yourself*)

178

5) Jesus, You really are the Son of God, the chosen One. I only wish to listen, to follow and to obey. Thank You for having sent Your Mother, Mary, in Your name to speak to me. She invites me to completely decide for You and, above all things, to consciously choose the Father and receive joy in doing so. She said:

"Dear children! Today, I invite You to decide for God once again and to choose Him before everything and above everything, so that He may work miracles in your life and so that, day by day, your life may become joy with Him. Therefore, little children, pray and do not permit Satan to work in your life through misunderstandings, non- understandings and non- acceptance of one another. Pray that you may be able to comprehend the greatness and the beauty of the gift of life. Thank you for having responded to my call." (January 25, 1990)

Jesus, be merciful to me today and do not keep from me the experience of Tabor. I have decided for the Father through You and in the Holy Spirit. Do not leave me in the darkness. Grant that I may look on the beauty of Your face. Deliver me from the works of Satan and all that hinders me from immersing myself in the beauty of Your presence. You know, Jesus, how far away from You my heart is. Today, I want to be near You. Do not allow me to be overpowered by spiritual drowsiness, as happened to Your apostles.

- Jesus, awaken me, so that I may recognize You, adore You and rejoice in and through You.
  (Repeat this invocation quietly within yourself)

179

6) Jesus, I adore and glorify You, because You revealed Yourself to Your Apostles on Tabor. Even though they did not quite understand what was happening, they realized that You were the chosen One. Their hearts were immersed in joy. Today, I adore You in the name of those who call You by name, but remain in the darkness of sin – without joy in their lives, without any real desire to be with You. I adore You, in the name of all those who have erected the tent of their lives far away from You, who avoid You or who fear You. I adore You, in the name of those who are spiritually ill or dead. O Jesus, they need a 'Tabor experience.' They need to see Your face, and to hear the Father's voice. Look on them all, Lord Jesus, because they are walking in darkness and cannot see or recognize the beauty of Your face.

(Reflect on and pray for those who no longer pray or practice their religion.)

7) Jesus, I adore You and I bless You, because You gave the experience of Tabor to Your Apostles. This gave them joy and an even greater desire to follow You. It was one of the experiences which helped and sustained them in their mission, and especially in moments of trial and suffering. Jesus, I present to You now our Pope, our bishops and especially priests and religious. Many of them are in spiritual crises or experience deep sadness and difficulties. Be merciful towards them and help them to recognize Your face. Let them feel joy in having met and followed You. May they fulfill their vocations with love and joy. Bless them as they are announcing Your Word, so that their faces may reflect Yours and their voices resonate that of the Father, so that You may be recognized

for what You really are: the Redeemer, the Savior, the Chosen One to whom we all must listen.
(In silence, reflect and pray for the Pope, your bishop, your parish priest, deacon and catechists.)

8) Jesus, I adore You and thank You for having revealed to us the sweetness of Your face and its splendor. It put new energy into the souls of Your Apostles. They wanted to remain on Tabor. Be blessed and praised in all those who have become witnesses of Your goodness and beauty. Be blessed and praised in every gentle and smiling person who restores our peace and trust in mankind. May their faces reflect Yours. Be blessed and praised in those faces which show hatred, dissatisfaction and anger. May the sweetness of Your face change their hearts. May Your face reflect on their faces so that they have Your glance of love, Your gentle face. I want to present to You in a special way those children who are exposed to tension and unrest, to the hatred and bitterness of their parents, and of those who educate them. You know how difficult it is to tolerate and undergo this type of behavior. It causes deep wounds. May all faces change into Yours, Jesus. May every glance become Your all-embracing glance of love, and may it be a source of healing for those who suffer.
(In silence, reflect on and present to Jesus those for whom you should pray at this moment!)

9) Jesus, I adore You and I thank You that Your prayer on Tabor teaches us something about prayer. Grant that we will love creation, that we will seek and love those solitary places, that we will set ourselves apart from the voices and sounds of the world to be alone with You.

Nature and creation speak of You. Increase our faith and love, so that we may meet You in all creatures and in all creation and, united with it, sing Your praises. May our hearts yearn for You and recognize Your love in every flower, in every tree, in every spring and in every rock. May our heart rejoice in all these things as a little child rejoices in the things that its father makes. Look down on all those who, by their way of life, have separated themselves from nature, and therefore, find it more difficult to open to You or to hear Your voice. Be blessed and praised because Your Mother here in Medjugorje invites us to Apparition Hill (Podbrdo) and Cross Mountain (Krizevac) because She wants us to look at nature and to learn from it:

"Dear children! I invite you to open yourselves to God. See, little children, how nature is opening itself and is giving life and fruits. In the same way, I invite you to live with God and to surrender completely to Him..."
(May 25, 1989)

Jesus, grant us the grace that, through the encounter with nature, we increasingly open ourselves to You and that, after every encounter, we return to the Church more ready and more capable to recognize You in the Eucharist and to look at Your face.

- Jesus, open my heart so that it can embrace life and bring forth fruit in the strength of Your spirit.
  (Repeat this invocation quietly within yourself)

10) Blessing

Jesus, show us now Your face. Bless us, illuminate us, give us happiness, heal us, so that Your face shines within us and that, through us, all may recognize You. Deliver us from all darkness. Bless all people and nations. Bless all that is created through You and is an image of Your immense goodness. Bless us all and grant that we may be with You, who lives and reigns world without end. Amen.

MOST HOLY TRINITY, I ADORE YOU

1) Good Father, Creator of all, I adore You!
   Son of the Father, Redeemer of all, I adore You.
   Holy Spirit who proceeds from the Father and the
   Son, I adore You.
   Most Holy Trinity, worthy of every thanks and
   praise, I adore You!

2) Jesus, while I adore You with the Father and the
Holy Spirit, I desire to immerse myself in the mystery of
divine life and feel its holiness and sublimity. The prophet
Isaiah helps me as he tells about Your call:

*"In the year of King Uzziah's death, I saw the Lord seated
on a high and lofty throne; His train filled the sanctuary. Above
Him stood Seraphs, each one with six wings: two to cover its face,
two to cover its feet and two for flying, and they were shouting these
words to each other : 'Holy, holy, holy, is Yahweh Sabaoth. His
glory fills the whole earth.' The door posts shook at the sound of
their shouting, and the Temple was full of smoke. Then I said:
'Woe is me, I am lost for I am a man of unclean lips and I live
among a people of unclean lips, and my eyes have seen the King,
Yahweh Sabaoth.' Then one of the Seraphs flew to me, holding in
its hand a live coal which it had taken from the altar with a pair of
tongs. With this, it touched my mouth and said: 'Look, this has
touched your lips, your guilt has been removed and your sin forgiven."*
(Is 6:1-7)
   - Holy, holy, holy, Lord God of Power and
   Might, Heaven and earth are full of Your glory!
   (Repeat this prayer quietly within yourself)

3) O Most Holy Trinity, I adore You and glorify You. I know that I am not worthy to praise and glorify You because of my sinfulness; therefore, I cannot now enter into the magnificence of Your holiness. My thoughts, words and actions have been unjust and loveless. I tarnish Your holiness and sublimity. I live among a people of unclean lips. Blasphemy, slander, lies and defaming the character of others, swearing and cursing are on the lips of almost all. We are not worthy to sing to You: "Holy, holy, holy!" Lord, purify the lips and the hearts of my people so that, from now on, we can breathe in Your majesty and worthily sing songs of Your praise and glory.

> -   Clean, my heart and soul, O Lord, purify my people so that together we may sing: holy, holy, holy!
> (*Repeat this prayer quietly within yourself*)

4) O mystery of the Most Holy Trinity, I adore You with all my heart and soul, my mind and my will. I now wish to immerse myself completely into the mystery of life and love – and also into the mystery of mercy and forgiveness. Jesus, drive out all that is hindering me from immersing myself completely in the mystery of Your life with the Father and the Holy Spirit. I do not wish to understand Your mystery, but to live within it. May my heart, together with the whole Church, now sing with You:

All hail adored Trinity,
All praise eternal unity,
O God the Father, God the Son,
And God the Spirit, three in One.

Three Persons praise we evermore,
And thee the Eternal One adore,
In Thy sure mercy everkind,
May we our true protection find.

O Trinity, O Unity,
Be present as we worship Thee,
And to the angels' songs in light
Our prayers and praises now unite.

Praise God from whom all blessings flow;
Praise Him all creatures here below;
Praise Him above ye heavenly host:
Praise Father, Son, and Holy Ghost.

> \- Father, Son and Holy Spirit, Most Holy
> Trinity, I adore You and I bless You.
> *(Repeat this quietly within yourself)*

5) Jesus, You spoke about the Father and the Holy Spirit. But those to whom You spoke did not understand what You were saying. They judged You because they could not understand the truth which You brought them that You were indeed in the Father and the Father in You. Jesus, the scribes and the Pharisees could not listen to You, they rejected and judged You because You had called Yourself the true Son of God. I believe that You are in the Father and the Father is in You. I know that the Holy Spirit is Your bond with the Father, I adore You through the mystery which St. Paul speaks about:

"*How rich and deep are the wisdom and the knowledge of God! We cannot reach to the root of His decisions or His ways. Who has ever known the mind of the Lord? Who has ever been His advisor? Who has given anything to Him, so that His presents come only as a debt returned? Everything there is comes from Him and is caused by Him and exists for Him. To Him be glory for ever and ever! Amen.*" (Rom 11:33-36)

>   -   To You, O Holy Trinity, be all praise for ever
>   and ever, Father, Son and Holy Spirit.
>   (*Repeat this prayer quietly within yourself*)

6)   Most Holy Trinity, Father, Son, and Holy Spirit, I adore You! I wonder at Your sublimity, Your depth and Your width, Your infinity and the eternity of Your being. Be blessed and praised because You have revealed Yourself to us in Your glory. Be blessed and praised because You dwell with us. You chose the hearts of mankind as a dwelling place, and You dwell in every church and oratory and in the whole of nature too.

Mary, You are the beloved daughter of the Father. Jesus, Your faithful Mother, betrothed of the Holy Spirit, teaches me and invited me to discover and accept personal holiness, to discover the sublimity of every church, because You dwell there:

"**Dear children! God wants to make you holy. Therefore, through me, He is inviting you to complete surrender. Let Holy Mass be your life. Understand that the church is God's palace, the place where I gather you and where I want to show you the way to God. Come and pray! Do not look at others or slander them, but rather, let your life be a testimony**

187

on the way of holiness. Churches are holy and deserve respect because God, who became man, dwells in them day and night. Therefore, little children, believe and pray that the Father increase your faith, and then seek whatever you need. I am with you and I am rejoicing because of your conversion and I am protecting you with my motherly mantle. Thank you for having responded to my call."
(April 25, 1988)

- Father, Son, and Holy Spirit, I adore You, here and in churches all over the world.

  (Repeat this prayer quietly within yourself)

7) Jesus, I adore You with the Father in the Holy Spirit. I wish to adore You night and day. I wish to comprehend with my whole heart that You, Most Holy Trinity, are present in all creation and in every person. May my heart exalt with joy and my soul sing in jubilee. May my body dance with enthusiasm and my whole life become a pure sign of Your presence. Free my heart from all other attachments so that You may be in the first place. Remove from me all false gods. Be blessed and praised, Jesus, in the Father and through the Holy Spirit, because You have chosen my body as a temple. Grant me the grace of a deep consciousness of this truth so that I live through it and in it.

-Father, Son and Holy Spirit, in You I live, I move and exist!

(Repeat this prayer quietly within yourself)

8)   Jesus, I adore You in the Father and in the Holy Spirit, with the heavens and the earth, all creation and all peoples. Father, I adore You in the name of those who do not know You, who reject Your son and who do not accept Your Holy Spirit. I fall on my knees in the name of those who have no knowledge of You, and in the name of those who recognize that You exist, but, in their hearts, have no faith or trust towards You, and so wander about this world, searching for love, peace and happiness – but find none. O Most Holy Trinity, reveal Yourself to them in Your fullness, in all Your splendor and glory, so that they may accept you and fall on their knees and shout for joy. Grant that from now on, every heart may be filled with happiness because it has opened up to You and become Your dwelling place. I praise You in the name of those who are responsible for the ignorance of you, who have distanced themselves from You, because sin and evil have led them away from You. May they receive the grace to discover You again as the foundation and security for their lives.

(Present those persons you know who are far away from God)

9)   Jesus, I praise You, with the Father in the Holy Spirit, in the name of my people. I praise You with all Christians who consciously live and accept Your presence and glorify Your love. I praise You with all those who are baptized and, by their baptism, have become temples of Your presence. And I praise You in the name of those who, through sin, have tainted You and even banished You from themselves. Grant that they return to You. I present to You in a special way those who curse and blaspheme You, defaming the sublimity of Your holiness,

and who are not completely conscious of what they are doing. I present to You those who do it just out of habit and have no idea what they are saying. I present to You also those who consciously defame and cure You. Liberate my people from the evil spirit of blasphemy and cursing, so that every heart may glorify and thank, bless and exalt You.

- Holy, holy, holy, Lord, God of Power and Might. Heaven and earth are full of Your glory! (Repeat this prayer quietly within yourself)

10) Blessing

Father, I pray to You in the name of Your Son Jesus Christ whom You sent, conceived by the Holy Spirit, to save us and deliver us. Heal us in heart and soul, so that our conscience and our subconscious are purified and we can be Your people, Your royal priesthood, Your holy nation. Father, this is what I ask in the name of Your Son Jesus in the Holy Spirit, who said to us: "whatever you ask in my name, the Father will give." May the blessing of the almighty God descend upon all of us here, on our families, on the Church and on the whole world that, through You, Jesus, was created, redeemed, and sanctified in the strength of the Spirit. You, who live and reign world without end. Amen.

JESUS, KING OF KINGS, I ADORE YOU

1) Jesus, I adore You, because You are the King of Kings!
Jesus, I love You, because you are the eternal Son of God, King of Peace!
Jesus, I believe in You, because You are the faithful King and You gave Your life for me.

2) O come let us adore Jesus Christ, King of Kings.
"Come, let us cry out with joy to Yahweh, acclaim the rock of our salvation.

Let us come into His presence with thanksgiving, acclaim Him with music.

For Yahweh is a great God, a king greater than all the Gods.

In His power are the depths of the earth, the peaks of the moutains are His;

The sea belongs to Him, for He made it, and the dry land molded by His hands.

Come, let us bow low and do reverence; kneel before Yahweh who made us!

For He is our God, and we the people of His sheepfold, the flock of His hand."
(Ps 95:1-7)

-   Come let us adore Jesus Christ, the King of Kings.
(Repeat this prayer quietly within yourself)

3) I will sing to You, Christ the King, together with the voices of Your Church:

Hail Redeemer King divine!
Priest and Lamb the throne is Thine
King whose reign shall never cease.
Prince of everlasting peace.

Angels, saints and nations sing,
Praised be Jesus Christ our King.
Lord of life, earth, sky and sea
King of love on Calvary.

King whose name creation thrills,
Rule our hearts our minds our wills
Till in peace each nation rings
With thy praises King of Kings.

King most holy King of Truth,
Guide the lowly guide the youth,
Christ Thou King of glory bright,
Be to us eternal light.

Shepherds King o'er mountains sleep,
Homeward bring the wandering sheep,
Shelter in our royal fold
States and kingdoms new and old.

(Remain in silence and repeat whatever part of the hymn appeals
particularly to you.)

4) Jesus, my King, I adore You with Mary, the
Queen, and with all the angels and saints. I adore You
with all creation which, one day, will be subject to Your
reign and Your power. St. Paul teaches us:

192

"For He is to be King until He has made his enemies a footstool, and the last of His enemies to be done away with is death, for he has put all things under his feet. But when it is said, everything is subjected , this obviously cannot include the one who subjected everything to Him. When everything has been subjected to Him then the Son Himself will be subjected to the One who has subjected everything to Him, so that God may be in all."
(1 Cor 15:25-28)

Jesus, my King, I now open my heart, together with Mary, and subject myself to Your power so that You reign in me just as You reigned in Her heart, and as You reign over all angels and saints. I want to listen and obey Her too, because She invites me to decide for and to abandon my life to You:

"Dear children! I call you to decide completely for God. I beseech you, dear children, to surrender yourselves completely and you shall be able to live everything I am telling you. It will not be difficult for you to surrender yourselves completely to God. Thank you for having responded to my call."
(January 2, 1986)

- Jesus, I open myself completely to You. Reign in my heart!

(Repeat this prayer quietly within yourself)

5) Jesus, my King, I honor and glorify You. I bless and exalt You because You are raised above all things. I want to offer my praises in reparation for all the offenses and humiliations that You experience from mankind from the beginning up until now. I want to offer it up for those insults which You will hear and suffer in the future from those very people for whom You gave Your life in total

love. I want to show appreciation for Your royal love towards me and in the name of all those who do not thank you. I want to honor and thank you in the name of Your people, Israel, who did not recognize You, but instead renounced You. St. John writes:

"So Pilate went back into the Praetorium and called Jesus to him and asked Him: 'Are you the King of the Jews?' Jesus replied: 'Do you ask this of your own accord or have others said it to you about me?' Pilate answered: 'Am I a Jew? It is your own people and the chief priests who have handed you over to me. What have you done?' Jesus replied: 'Mine sis not a kingdom of this world; if my kingdom were of this world, my men would have fought to prevent my being surrendered to the Jews. As it is, my kingdom does not belong here.' Pilate said: 'So then, you are a king?' Jesus answered: 'It is you who say that I am a king. I was born for this, to bear witness to the truth; and all who are on the side of truth listen to my voice.'" (Jn 18:33-37)

> - Jesus, You are my King whom I recognize, praise and exalt!
>
> *(Repeat this prayer quietly within yourself)*

6) Jesus, my King, I adore and thank You because You announced the kingdom of justice, truth and love, and because Your kingdom is eternal. I bless you, because You have won the victory over the kingdom of evil and sin, the kingdom of the prince of this world, and You have destroyed his power and might. Your people misjudged You, saying that You did what you did with the power of Satan, and that You serve his kingdom. Thank You for the answer which St. Mark writes:

"The scribes who had come down from Jerusalem were saying: 'Beelzebul is in him,' and 'It is through the prince of devils that he drives devils out.' So He called them to Him and spoke to them in parables: 'How can Satan drive out Satan?' If a kingdom is divided against itself that kingdom cannot last. And if a household is divided against itself that household will never last."
(Mk 3:22-25)

Lord Jesus, King of Goodness, in Your name I now renounce the kingdom of evil and sin. Deliver me from the deeds of Satan, and grant me the grace to always recognize his deeds so that I may reject them. Forgive me for the past in which I have consciously or unconsciously cooperated with the kingdom of evil. With the help of Your grace, I will never do so again. I wish to be completely free for Your kingdom. To You, my King, belongs first priority in my words, my thoughts, my deeds and my whole life. I renounce all bondage to sin and I accept gratefully the freedom which You give to Your followers.

(Offer your heart now in silence to the Lord and ask Him to drive far from you all bondage and all attachments which keep Him from having the first place in your life.)

7) Jesus, my King, be blessed because You led a life of simplicity, love, respect and obedience to Your parents, Mary and Joseph. I bless and praise You, Jesus, because You lived Your celestial and divine royalty hidden in the obscurity of a family home. Be blessed, because You wish to be King of our families. Thank You because You offer us the help of Your love, mercy and forgiveness. But Your reigning is serving.

O Jesus, be King of our family. May every fatherly and motherly heart breathe in Your spirit and, with Your love, serve life in their families. There where pride, jealousy, envy, selfishness, drunkenness, atheism, mistrust and lies are reigning, where family members want to dominate rather than serve each other, may Your Spirit of love and humility, and readiness for self-sacrifice, renew families today and be their salvation! May our families be Your Kingdom of truth, justice, love, peace, life and joy. Liberate them, Jesus, from all evil so that all our families and all their members become completely Yours! May Your love reign in them. May life reign within them, and may they be victorious over death. Grant, that Your kingdom be firmly established in our families and that, in every family, You be glorified and praised.

(In silence, present your family to the Lord and the families of those you know, particularly those in difficulty!)

8) Jesus, King of Kings, I bless and praise You, in Your Church that You left to this world to continue Your work of salvation in the strength of the same Spirit in which You worked. All this was for the expansion of Your kingdom for which You gave Your life. I adore You today, together with all those who will sing to their Most High King, and I thank You that many today will solidify their faith, reminded that they belong to You, and You to them. I thank You because their surrendering to You aids the victory of Your kingdom.

Be blessed also for all those who, today in churches are there in body only or who are spiritually dead, because You will give them the grace today to feel the beauty once again of Your reign, and the happiness of belonging to You. Remove from them all influence of evil, and grant that they live in the freedom of the children of God which only You can give.

Be blessed and praised for those who, through the Apostles, were entrusted with important roles in Your Church. Reign in a special way in the hearts, minds, words and deeds of the Pope, the bishops, the priests and religious and all those who announce the Gospel. May Your Church today become Your reign – without stain or wrinkle, united in love and faithful to the will of the Father. Purify Your Church, Jesus, so that it can worthily sing Your praises today:

"It is truly right and fitting to give thanks always and everywhere to You Lord, Almighty God and Father. With the oil of exaltation, You consecrated Your only Son, Our Lord, Jesus Christ, as eternal Priest and King of the Universe. On the altar of the Cross, He sacrifices Himself as the immaculate victim of peace, and consummates the mystery of human redemption; rendering all creatures subject to His power and offers to Your infinite majesty the eternal and universal reign: the reign of truth and life, the reign of eternal grace, the reign of justice, of love and of peace. …" (From the Liturgy of the Hour – Solemnity of Christ the King)

(Reflect in silence on the words you have just read)

9) Jesus, King of all creation, King of Heaven and earth, thank You for wishing to redeem the world into one big family. Be blessed because there is a place in Your kingdom for sinners and sick people, for the scorned and the rejected. Thank You, Jesus, that You reject no-one, not even those who reject You. I adore You, and I desire that all people meet You. Reveal Yourself to all, so that all

will be saved in order that all may glorify You in the future.

(Remain in silence and pray for the conversion of your family and friends, for your nation and the whole world, especially those who are in crises of faith.)

10) Blessing

Jesus, I adore You and I believe in Your love towards the sick and the disabled. Only say Your royal, divine, almighty Word and drive away and deliver us from all evil. Calm the restless. Fill with love those who live with hatred within. Restore Your justice to where injustice reigns today. Replace un-forgiveness with forgiveness and return life to wherever death has cast its shadow. Liberate all people who are now under bondage of evil and sin. May Your royal blessing fall upon us all, on every nation in the Holy Spirit, in which You live and reign world without end. Amen.

JESUS, I CAME TO THANK YOU

1) Jesus, I adore You because You constantly thanked the Father.
Jesus, I love You, because You taught me how to thank.
Jesus, I believe in You, because You have the Word of eternal life.

2) Jesus, I adore You and, today, I wish to learn to give thanks, I wish to accept Your invitation to be always thankful. Send Your Holy Spirit into my heart! May He teach me thankfulness, may He purify me from my pride and from any hindrance to the Father's will, so that I may always give thanks, even for things which are more difficult to accept. I do not wish to be blind or forgetful. I wish to be able to see clearly all I have that comes from the Father's hand, and to thank Him humbly for it. St. Luke writes:

"Now it happened that on the way to Jerusalem, He was traveling on the borderlands of Samaria and Galilee. As He entered one of the villages, ten men suffering of a virulent skin disease came to meet Him. They stood some way off, and called to Him: 'Jesus, Master, take pity on us.' When He saw them, He said: 'Go and show yourselves to the priests.' Now as they were going away, they were cleansed. Finding himself cured, one of them turned back praising God at the top of his voice and threw himself prostrate at the feet of Jesus and thanked Him. The man was a Samaritan. This led Jesus to say: 'Were not all ten made clean? The other nine, where are they? It seems that no-one came back to give praise to God, except this foreigner!" (Lk 17:11-18)

Father, on my knees now like the Samaritan, I wish to thank You for every time I forgot or refused to give thanks. I wish to thank You for all those times when I attributed the glory to myself instead of to You. Forgive my ungratefulness and accept now my words: Thank You, thank You, my Jesus! May gratitude spring out form my heart and cleanse if from every bitterness or anger at the Father's will! May I continually thank You as I kneel before You.

    -   Jesus, I thank the Father through You and for all Your grace and goodness!

3) Jesus, I adore You and I wish to thank You with Mary. O Mary, how thankful You were because You were the chosen One, because in humility, You recognized God's work in You and You thanked Him. When Elisabeth greeted You and called You blessed among women, You sang out a prayer: "My soul magnifies the Lord and my spirit rejoices in God my Savior!" O how thankful Your heart was and, being thankful, it was joyful and being joyful, it was trustful. Thank you, Mary, because in Your message, You invite me:

"Dear children! I wish to tell you to thank God for all the graces which God has given you. For all the fruits, thank the Lord and glorify Him! Dear children, learn to give thanks in little things and then you will be able to give thanks for the big things. Thank you oft having responded to my call."
(October 3, 1985)

Mary, I want to rejoice before the Lord with You and, in silence, let my soul sing, thank, glorify and praise.

Teach me, O Mary, to be thankful, just as every mother teaches her child.

> -   Jesus, my soul now thanks and rejoices in You because You have done wonders for me too!
>
> *(Repeat this prayer quietly within yourself)*

4) Father, Creator of the world, Jesus, the Redeemer, and Holy Spirit, illuminate my soul. I adore You and thank You because You allow me to call myself a child of God. Father, thank You because You are, because You exist, because You love, because You forgive, because You watch over and care for me. Jesus, thank You because You gave Your life for me and remained in the Eucharist. Holy Spirit, thank You because You inspire, renew and guide me, because you are the Spirit of truth, of love of justice and of peace.

How ashamed I am now that I sometimes found prayer so hard, so boring, because my heart was closed. How ashamed I am now, because I so often said the Our Father, never thinking what a privilege it is to be Your child, in sorrow and in joy, in success and failure, in health and sickness.

I always have a reason to be joyful. From now on, I wish with all my heart and all my soul to be thankful – thankful that I can pray, because it is a great gift. I thank You for the gift of my life, for my baptism, for holy communion and confirmation, for every confession and for all the graces that You have given me. Thank You for my past which I commend to Your mercy, my future which I commend to Your love and my present in which, by Your grace, I can do good.

- Jesus, I thank the Father through You for my life and all that happens with me!
  (Repeat this prayer quietly within yourself)

5) Jesus, today I kneel before You and I wish to thank You with all my heart for my family. You were always thankful to Mary, Your Mother, for having said: "Here I am Lord, may it be done unto me according to Thy Word." Without this, You Jesus, would not have been able to come into this world or to redeem it. Therefore, while I thank the Father through You for Your life, I wish today to consciously thank You for my mother and my father. Blessed be that moment when they said 'yes' to life! Blessed be that time that I spent in my mother's womb! I thank You, Jesus, because it was with the help of Your grace that they accepted me and educated me.

(In silence, present and thank the Lord for your parents)

As I remain before You now I want to forgive my mother and father for all that I expected of them, but they were unable to offer me and, as a result, I remained wounded and disillusioned.

(Reflect on the misunderstandings and on the family conflicts, on the times when your behavior made life difficult for your parents. Repent, forgive and seek forgiveness from God with the intention of seeking it from those you have offended.)

- Jesus, I thankfully accept my life and I thank You for my parents.
  (Repeat this prayer quietly within yourself)

6)   Jesus, I adore You and I thank You because You wish to give Your peace to every family. But I know that there can be no joy and no communion if children are not thankful to their parents or if parents do not appreciate their children.   I know how souls carry the wounds throughout their entire earthly life if they do not receive love and are not accepted with joy as children. May the Spirit of thankfulness be poured into every heart and may it heal the wounds that damage family relationships. May those who are now in danger of rejecting life, receive the grace to accept it. Thank You, Jesus, that You love and accept each one of us, especially if we have been rejected by someone.   Thank You, because Your love heals wounds, gives peace, happiness and contentment.
(Reflect on and present to the Lord those who are in trials, especially the unwanted or aborted children, or those who were abandoned after birth.)

7)   Jesus, I adore You and I thank You today for placing me in the community of the Church. Blessed be that moment when my parents brought me to be baptized and I became part of the community of saints. I want a great consciousness to grow within me now of how I am in communion with You, so that I can gratefully accept divine life and Your gifts, and thankfully take care of them. I know that many have abandoned Your invitation and live as if they never knew You and as if You never invited them to be in communion with You.   May gratitude for their baptisms now fill their hearts and possess them completely. I adore You and I thank You, together with them, who are conscious that they have come from the darkness into the light and from death to

203

life through their baptisms. Lord Jesus, may Your gratitude grow within them. St. Paul writes:

> *"I am continually thanking God for you, for the grace of God which you have been given in Christ Jesus; in Him you have been richly endowed in every type of utterance and knowledge; so firmly has witness to Christ taken root in you. And so you are not lacking in any gift as you wait for our Lord, Jesus Christ, to be revealed; He will continue to give you strength till the very end, so that you will be irreproachable on the day of Our Lord Jesus Christ."* (1 Cor 1:4-9)

- Jesus, thank You because You make me strong in faith, hope and love.

(Repeat this prayer quietly within yourself)

8) Jesus, I adore You and I want to thank You for all the good and all the graces for which I never showed appreciation. I especially want to thank You for all those trials and difficulties which happened to me. Sometimes they made me doubt the love and goodness of the Father. Forgive me that my crosses and sufferings led me far away from You and destroyed all joy and gratitude in my heart. I bring before You now all those moments of trial and doubt and I believe that You can turn everything to good an dot the glory of the Father. I now place before You all those moments of suffering in my past, my present and my future and I thank You because I know now that my life is in Your hands, and that, even when I make mistakes, You can bring it all to good in the moment when I come asking for forgiveness and promising to try to be better.

(Reflect on and offer up all those moments of your life when bitterness pierced your soul, and anger and mistrust towards God filled you and perhaps you experienced even hatred or fear.)

9) Jesus, I adore You and I thank You now for all the people who are suffering and who are living tragedies, especially the innocent, the abandoned, the excluded, the sick and the elderly. I thank You, Jesus, because I know that it is possible for You to turn it to good and to the glory of the Father. Thank You, Jesus, because You lead everything to eternal life in justice and love. I know present to You all the bitterness, fear and pain of those who are suffering and who, because of this, rebel against the Father, those who, when in suffering, curse and swear instead of humbly saying: "Father, may Your will be done!"

(Reflect in silence on those who are now in difficulty and, as a result, are in danger of losing their faith and love.)

10) Blessing

Jesus, while I thank the Father and the Holy Spirit, I invoke Your mercy in the words of St. Paul:

"Blessed be the God and Father of our Lord Jesus Christ, the merciful Father and the God who gives every possible encouragement; He supports us in every hardship so that we are able to come to the support of others in every hardship of theirs because of the encouragement that we ourselves receive from God."
(2 Cor 1:3-4)

May Your encouragement and Your peace, and the Spirit of thankfulness descend upon us, fill our hearts, heal us from all ills and grant us eternal peace. Amen.

JESUS, I ADORE YOU,
DELIVER ME FROM ALL EVIL

1) I adore You, Jesus, because You liberate from sin.
   I love You, Jesus, because You give interior freedom.
   I believe in You, Jesus, because You have the victory over sin and death.

2) Jesus, I adore You, together with Mary, because She was the first to experience the strength of Your grace, because She was protected from all stain of sin even before the beginning of Her existence. I praise You and glorify You because, in Her, You want me to see myself as I could be. Thank You, because You send Her to guide me. She tells me:

"Dear children! Today, I want to wrap you all in my mantle and lead you all along the way of conversion. Dear children, I beseech you, surrender to the Lord your entire past, all the evil that has accumulated in your hearts. I want each one of you to be happy but, in sin, nobody can be happy. Therefore, dear children, pray and, in prayer, you shall realize a new way of joy. Joy will manifest itself in your hearts and thus you shall be joyful witnesses of what I and my Son want from each one of you. I am blessing you. Thank you for having responded to my call." (February 25, 1987)

Father, in the name of Your Son, Our Lord Jesus Christ, in the Holy Spirit, I beseech You, together with Your Mother Mary, to deliver me from the sins of my past. I abandon all to You. Deliver me so that, in this very moment, I may be completely freed. Jesus, You cut all possible bonds with sin and evil and heal all wounds left from sin – even original sin. My heart can now be freed from evil and will be able to feel deep joy. Deliver me from all evil so that I can feel that freedom that only You give.

(Reflect on your life and offer to Jesus all that weighs you down, especially sinful and bad habits)

3) Jesus, I adore You because You have the victory over Satan and because You have unmasked his deeds. Be blessed and praised because, when Satan was making someone suffer, just one word from You was enough to drive him out. I thank You for Your response to Satan when he tempted You during Your fast in the desert. St. Matthew tells us:

"Then Jesus was led by the Spirit out into the desert to be put to the test by the devil. He fasted for forty days and forty nights after which He was hungry, and the tester came and said to Him: 'If you are the Son of God, tell those stones to turn into loaves.' But He replied: 'Scripture says: human beings live not on bread alone, but on every word which comes from the mouth of God.' The devil then took Him to the holy city and set Him on the parapet of the Temple. 'If you are the Son of God,' he said, 'throw yourself down for Scripture says: he has given His angels orders about You, and they will carry You in their Arms in case You trip over a stone. Jesus said to him: 'Scripture also says: Do no put the Lord your God to the test.' Next, taking Him to a very high mountain, the devil showed Him all the kingdoms of the world and their splendor. And he said to Him: 'I will give you all these if you fall at my feet and do me homage.' Then Jesus replied: 'Away with you Satan! For Scripture says: The Lord your God is the one to whom you must do homage,

Him alone you must serve.' Then the devil left Him and suddenly angels appeared and looked after Him." (Mt 4:1-11)

Jesus, I want to be always with You and always know the way to drive Satan away. I want to decide completely for You, because You speak the Word of God, because You give strength and power and You do not test the Father but serve Him with Your whole being. Forgive me for having given in to temptation. In Your name, I renounce Satan and his deeds, and I chose the freedom of the children of God.

- Jesus, Lord God, I wish to serve You and adore only You!

(Repeat this prayer quietly within yourself)

4) Jesus, I adore You, because you are the Son of God, because You have the victory and because salvation comes only in Your name. Only You give that real joy to those who are with You, to those who pray. Be blessed and praised because Mary, too, in Your name invites and warns:

"Dear children! In these days you have experienced God's sweetness through the renewals in this parish. Satan wants to work still more fiercely to take away the joy from each one of you. By prayer, you can completely disarm him and ensure your happiness. Thank you for having responded to my call." (January 24, 1985)

Mary, I promise You now in front of Jesus that I will pray and so, together with You, will have the victory over evil, sin, Satan and his wicked deeds. I believe that You are protecting me and that You will continue to do so. You spread Your mantle over me so that Satan can

208

have no influence over me and You will alert me and, in the strength of the Holy Spirit., I will turn my back on all his insinuations.

> \- Jesus, I adore You with Mary and I decide for collaboration with You in the battle against evil!
> (*Repeat this prayer quietly within yourself*)

5) Jesus, victorious One, I adore You and glorify Your victory over Satan, the conceiver of every sin, because You give us Your interior freedom. As I thank You for freeing me and for giving me faith in Your power, I offer up to You my family, my parish community, my church and Your people and the whole world. You only have to say the Word and You will deliver us from Satan's deeds and his collaborators. St. Peter invites us:

"Keep sober and alert, because your enemy, the devil, is on the prowl like a roaring lion looking for someone to devour. Stand up to him, strong in faith and in the knowledge that it is the same kind of suffering that the community of your brothers throughout the world is undergoing." (1 Pet 5:8-9)

Jesus, deliver the world from Satan's works. May nobody become a victim of his deeds anymore and may the whole world serve only You, Jesus. May nothing else and no one else be the cause of slavery to him, and may no one open the door for Satan's works again. Liberate all who are under the influence of Satan and all who have consciously given themselves over to him and to the service of evil. Free all those who, under his influence, have started on the road to drugs, alcoholism, injustice, sexual immorality, theft, murder, violence. Free those who have become members of occult practices, those who defile and make a sacrilege of Your Eucharistic love and those who participate in black masses.

- Jesus, only say the Word and deliver the world from Satanic works!

(Repeat this prayer quietly within yourself)

6) Jesus, I adore You and I thank You because You came to free the world from conflict and war, from the spirit of violence and the destruction of life. And You, too, became the victim of violence, they killed You and hung You on the cross! But Your heart was never overshadowed by evil or did the desire for revenge enter Your feelings. Instead, in the most difficult moment of Your suffering, You forgave. Thank You, because You are the master of every heart and every soul. Only say the Word and they will receive the gift of forgiveness. May all those who are victims have the strength to forgive, and those who have become offenders, may they become possessed by the Spirit of peacemaking. May every heart and soul now sing with the Psalmist:

"*Sing a new song to Yahweh, for He has performed wonders,*
His saving power is in His right hand and His holy arm,
Yahweh has made known His saving power, revealed His saving
justice for the nations to see, mindful of His faithful love
and His constancy to the House of Isael.
The whole wide world has seen the saving power of our God.
Acclaim Yahweh, all the earth, burst into shouts of joy!
Play to Yahweh on the harp, to the sound of instruments; to the
sound of trumpet and horn, acclaim the presence of the
King.
Let the sea thunder, and all that it holds, the world and all who
live in it.

Let the rivers clap their hands and the mountains shout for joy together at Yahweh's approach, for He is coming to judge the world with saving justice and the nations with fairness."
(Ps 98:1-9)

(Reflect on these words, and with your soul, sing together with all creation!)

7) Jesus, I adore You and I thank You because You lived in the Holy Family with Mary and Joseph. Harmony, love and reciprocal respect reigned and a divine peace prevailed as nothing could threaten it because Your hearts were free of any jealousy, envy, selfishness, doubt, injustice or lack of respect and appreciation for others.

I now bring before You all the sufferings of our families because they have lost that freedom internally, thereby becoming slaves of alcohol, drugs, atheism, jealousy and envy. Sometimes young people have no tolerance for the old, or the healthy will not tolerate the sick; this happens because all are wounded and relationships between them are destroyed. May our families become aware and accept what St. Paul says:

"After all, brothers, you were called to be free; do not use your freedom as an opening for self-indulgence, but be servants to one another in love, since the whole of the Law is summarized in the one commandment: 'You must love your neighbor as yourself.' If you go snapping at one another and tearing one another to pieces, take care; you will be eaten up by one another. Instead, I tell you, be guided by the Spirit, and you will no longer yield to self-indulgence. The desires of self-indulgence are always in opposition to the Spirit, and the desires of the Spirit are in opposition to self-indulgence: they are opposites, one against the other; that is how you are prevented from

doing the things you want to. But when you are led by the Spirit you are not under the Law." (Gal 5:13-18)

- Jesus, may our families be liberated from all that leads us into temptation, and may they be filled with Your Spirit. May we serve one another in love!

(Present Your family and families you know, especially those who are facing trials.)

8) Jesus, You wished for Your Church to be free and, in freedom, to serve the coming of Your kingdom. I thank You and I adore You because You wish to fill us with a new Spirit, to free us from all slavery to the laws of this world. Enable it to follow the laws of the Spirit. I present to You now all the division, the misunderstandings, the injustices the schisms and the discord which happen in the Church and through the Church in the world today. I present to You all the division between the Christian Churches and the slavery to false ideas and the desire for power. I present to You now all those times through the history of the Church when division was brewing with her, when the Christian community carried out acts, forgetting that one commandment which You gave: the commandment to love. I present to You all those moments when the power to dominate became more important, when factions and partisanship were the important issues, when, within the Church, people were weighed up according to non-Christian values.

May the words of Your apostle Paul give birth to a new Spirit of community and freedom in love:

"There are many gifts, but it is always the same Spirit; there are many different ways of serving, but it is always the same Lord. There are many different forms of activity, but in every body it is the same God who is at work in them all. The particular manifestation of the Spirit granted to each one is to be used for the general good." (1 Cor 12:4-7)

(Present your parish community, your local church and the whole Catholic Church and all other Christian communities to the Lord.)

9) Jesus, I adore and thank You for coming to deliver us. You know how many young people today are addicted to drugs, alcohol, to playing machines, gambling, to sexual immorality. In this way, they are ruining their personal and their Christian dignity. They suffer, their parents suffer, the Church suffers and the whole nation suffers. I beseech You today to illuminate those who, for money, lead young people to their ruin. Deliver them and also give them the strength to stop their evil behavior. Say the Word and grant them that inner freedom. Bless all those who sacrifice themselves to help the addicted. May their work with the addicted be successful so that every heart and soul can offer itself in freedom to You – its deliverer. *(In silence, present those you know who have these or similar problems)*

10) Blessing
Heavenly Father, in the name of Jesus, Your Son, the Redeemer and Deliverer, I beg You with Mary, the Queen of Peace, bless us all, all families and all peoples and nations. Put a stop to all slavery to evil and sin, and make people capable of freedom to love for another. Grant us

213

the gift of Your freedom so that we may all bear witness to Your goodness and love in the Holy Spirit, You who live and reign world without end. Amen.

JESUS, KING OF THE PROPHETS
I ADORE YOU

1) Jesus, I adore You, because You are the King of Prophets.
Jesus, I believe in You, because You gave Your life as a trustworthy witness to the Father's love.
Jesus, I love You, because You spoke in the name of the Father in the Holy Spirit.

2) Jesus, thank You because you came in the Father's name to speak to us in His name and so to fulfill the prophets' mission. That is why Your Word was: "Convert and believe in the Gospel!" That is why You had no fear in telling the truth, in doing justice and in always loving and forgiving. You really are the Prophet and King of all Prophets, because You were not afraid to give Your life, because You did not care for human prestige, You did no fear rejection or derision nor the death on a cross. Neither wealth, nor prestige, nor power could impose themselves upon You, even though these are the things which destroy the Spirit of a prophet. You remained faithful to the Father's will right up to the end. I adore You and I bless and praise You. You said:

"Truly, truly I say to you, the Son can do nothing without the Father, He can only do what He sees the Father doing; and whatever the Father does, the Son does too. For the Father loves the Son and shows Him everything He himself does, and He will show Him even greater things than these, works that will astonish you." (Jn 5:19-20)

- Jesus, King of Prophets, Victim of Truth, for Justice and Love, I adore You!

(Repeat this prayer quietly within yourself)

3) Jesus, I adore You today in the company of all the believers, all the faithful of the Old and New Testament who courageously fulfilled the prophetic calling. I adore You, together with them, because they too spoke in the name of the Father, they were invited to conversion, to prayer and fasting and announced peace. They announced chastisement, too, if the people did not convert. I adore You with Isaiah, Jeremiah, Ezekiel, Daniel, Joel, Amos and many others whom Your Spirit invited to speak and to announce His Words. In the strength of the Spirit, they went to kings and heads of state, to those who were responsible in society and in the synagogue, and invited them to renounce sin and evil, to return to the One and True God. And, for this, they were struck, imprisoned and killed. I adore You, together with them, because they announced Your coming. Jesus, be blessed for all those who changed their lives because of their words and converted.

(Remain in silence and deepen your awareness of your communion with the prophets of the Old Testament and open your heart up to the Spirit of Prophecy.)

4) I adore You, Jesus, together with St. John the Baptist, who prepared the way in the hearts of men for You. He recognized the messiah in You and he showed this to others. With strength, he announced the need for conversion and He lost his life because he had the fortitude and determination to also correct the king. St. Matthew tells us:

"Now it was Herod who had arrested John, chained him up and put him in prison because of Herodias, his brother Philip's wife. For John had told him: 'It is against the Law for you to have

216

her.' He had wanted to kill him, but was afraid of the people, who regarded John as a prophet. Then, during the celebrations for Herod's birthday, the daughter of Herodias danced before the company and so delighted Herod that he promised an oath to give her anything she asked. Prompted by her mother, she said: 'Give me John the Baptist's head here on a plate.'" (Mt 14:3-8)

Jesus, be blessed and praised for the strength and courage of St. John the Baptist and all the prophets of the New Testament, who, in Your Spirit, prophesied and announced Your reign of justice and love. Jesus, may my heart rejoice in You, King of Prophets. May it rejoice with all prophets, who joyfully fulfilled their callings. From now on, I wish to be conscious of my communion with them through You in the Holy Spirit.

(Open your heart further to be workings of the Holy Spirit)

5) Jesus, I adore You and I thank You that, through baptism, You invite me into communion with You. You have made me a member of Your Church and You have given Your Spirit of prophecy to me too that I may speak in Your name. I thank You for all those times when I felt the importance and had the courage to speak out for truth, justice and love. Be blessed and praised, Jesus, for all those times when I was made to suffer for having spoken out. I also present to You, Lord, all those times when fear and a desire for human respect held me back, when I did not speak in Your name and betrayed truth, justice and love. Purify me today, render me capable and fill me with Your Spirit so that, from now on, I will never back away from occasions to defend Your kingdom. May the Spirit which led the prophets inspire and lead me.

- Jesus, I adore You and I thank You because I am a member of Your prophetic people!
  (*Repeat this prayer quietly within yourself*)

6) Jesus, I adore and thank You because You were obedient to Mary and Joseph. They fulfilled the Father's will, educating You, looking after and caring for You. All that they did, they did as prophets, because they spoke and worked in the name of the Father. Be blessed and praised, Jesus, in all parents who untiringly and in the strength of Your Spirit, educate their children, giving them a good example and speaking to them in Your name. Grant them the strength to continue to be prophets at all times. May their words, through the grace of the Holy Spirit, take root in the hearts of their children to bring forth abundant fruit! May teachers, educators, catechists and professors be abundantly blessed because people place great trust in them. May all those in the public eye work with the Spirit of Prophecy, so that they lead and strongly advocate the truth as a value to be respected and served. May they battle against malignity, deception and grant that they do not compromise with sin, nor collaborate with evil. May all those who are in the political world be illuminated by the Prophetic Spirit, and worthily fulfill their role, battling without fear for just and truth. Grant that the desire for power, money and prestige does not corrupt their hearts and souls:

Forgive all parents, educators, and those responsible in our countries, when, out of fear, they collaborated with falsehood, injustice and force. Heal all the wounds, Jesus, and make my people into a prophetic people.

(In silence, meditate and present to Jesus your parents, educators, and all those in power.)

7)   Jesus, I adore and thank You for the gift of Your Prophetic Spirit to the Church and for having sent it to live and announce Your truth. In this way, we can battle against the spirit of lies effectively. Inspire our Pope, our bishops and our priests, so that they may guide, warn and invite to conversion and reconciliation without fear of testifying, because they are full of Your Spirit. May their hearts be pure and free from any evil or sin so that the Spirit of Prophecy may work openly within them! Be blessed in all those who do not say what everyone wants to hear, but who hunger for what You wish to be said. Grant that they may never fall prey to false teachings; instead may they decidedly uphold and announce the truth! May that happen what St. Paul writes for Timothy:

"Until I arrive, devote yourself to reading to the people, encouraging and teaching. You have in you a spiritual gift which was given to you when the prophets spoke and the body of elders laid their hands on you; do not neglect it. Let this be your care and your occupation, and everyone will be able to see your progress. Be conscientious about what you do and what you teach; persevere in this, and in this way you will save both yourself and those who listen to you!" (1 Tim 4:13-16)

(Pray for your parish priest, your confessor, your bishop, your teachers and the students in seminaries!)

8)   Jesus, I adore You because You came to bring truth and gave it to the Church through the Apostles, trusting us to keep watch and guard over it. Be blessed for

all those who live like prophets and proclaim the fullness of truth. Make all hearts open up to truth, those who teach and those who listen. St. Paul warned Timothy:

"*You may be quite sure that in the last days there will be some difficult times. People will be self-centered and avaricious, boastful, arrogant and rude, disobedient to their parents, ungrateful, irreligious; heartless and intractable; they will be slanderers, profligates and enemies of everything that is good; they will be treacherous and reckless and demented with pride, preferring their own pleasure to God. They will keep up the outward appearance of religion but will have rejected the inner power of it. Keep away from people like that.*" (2 Tim 3:1-5)

Jesus, I present to You all the false prophets of our times and all who follow them. May Your Holy Spirit be poured into their hearts and illuminate them. Deliver the Church and the world from all false teachings, ideologies and faiths, so that Your Church becomes immaculate, without stain or wrinkle.

(Reflect on your way of thinking and what it was that put you back on the right path, and whether you can help others to discover the truth too.)

9) Jesus, I adore You and I wish to pray for those who have wandered in their faith and no longer believe in Your Eucharistic presence. I wish to intercede for those who reject Your Mother, who have wandered from the teachings of the Church and do not accept the Pope. I present to You now all Christian communities who argue among themselves. I recommend to You all prayer groups who are under the guidance of false prophets and false visionaries and who spread fear and mistrust. I present to You all who knock down the pillars of morality set up by

Your Church. I present to You all sects, who chose from the revealed Word what appeals to them but reject what is uncomfortable. Send Your Holy Spirit to them, awaken the prophets in Your Church, those who teach, preach and guide so that they teach Your truth in its fullness. *(Reflect on those you have met who have diluted or diminished their faith and pray especially for them.)*

10) Blessing

Jesus, King of Prophets, You are the way, the truth, and the life. In Your name, I pray to the Father in the Holy Spirit with Mary, the Queen of Peace, to bless me and heal me, to guide and illuminate us, our families, the Church and the world. May Your Spirit inspire us fully and renew our whole lives and protect and guide us along Your path, You who live and reign world without end. Amen.

JESUS, I ADORE YOU, HEAL MY LOVE

1) Jesus, I adore You, because You alone are eternal
and infinite love!
Jesus, I believe in You, because You loved until
the end and gave Your life for us!
Jesus, I love You, because You are love, worthy of
every love.

2) Jesus, I thank You because You alone are love and
You taught that love is the only law. You said: "Love God
above all else and love your neighbor as yourself." Jesus, I
thank You for having loved me and for having revealed
the Father's eternal love to me, which is all-forgiving.
Grant that I may immerse myself ever deeper into the
Father's love through You. I realize that my heart is cold
and without real love for You or for the Father. Send me
Your Holy Spirit to set my heart aflame with divine love,
so that it may burn with love for the Father through You.
May my heart constantly contemplate You and beat with
great joy at the thought of You. Forgive me that my love
is so weak.

- Jesus, heal my love towards the Father by the
power of the Holy Spirit.
(Repeat this invocation quietly within yourself)

3) Jesus, You invite me to love my neighbor as
myself. Thank You for this invitation. I admit that it has
been difficult to love myself too. I know that I sometimes
did not accept myself as I am, that I ignored the gifts the
Father gave me and that often I was envious of others
because I believed that I do not have enough gifts. I

thought that I had been forgotten. Forgive me that I was tempted at times to not appreciate my life, to doubt the importance of my existence, because I know now that I wounded You deeply in Your love, in Your justice and mercy.

Send me Your Holy Spirit now so that He can purify my heart from all negative experiences in my life. Purify me from all the consequences of feeling unloved, because that hindered me from being able to love myself. Purify me so that, from now on, I may rejoice in my life and respond with love and joy to the challenges of every day. Forgive me for having damaged myself with my sins. Heal me Jesus!

- Jesus, teach me to love myself the way You love me!

(Present your life to Jesus, thank Him for all the good and the positive, together with all the trials, the problems and the crosses that you have carried or may still be carrying.)

4) Jesus, I adore and thank You because You invite me to love my neighbor as myself. I wish to decide now for love towards my neighbor, my family, towards my mother and father, towards my brothers and sisters. I wish to love all those whom I will meet, and those with whom I work and live. Grant me the gift of Your Holy Spirit so that I can be cleansed from all selfishness, pride, jealousy and envy. Heal me of my fear of others and of all wounds which I carry in my heart because of a lack of love in my childhood. Grant me the strength to forgive and that I may recognize You and love You in others. I admit that my type of love for my neighbor has only been a desire to dominate, impress or to use them, and that I

often disappointed my neighbor and made it difficult for him to love me accept me.

(Reflect on your relationship with your neighbors, forgive, and pray for them! If you have problems with anyone of them, pray particularly for them.)

> \- Jesus, eternal love, heal my love toward my neighbor!
>
> *(Repeat this invocation quietly within yourself)*

5) Jesus, thank You because You loved Your enemies, those who did not accept You, those who rejected you, who sought to put an end to Your life and succeed in crucifying you. Thank You because You invite me to love my enemies, to forgive, to bless them and to pray for them. St. Luke writes:

> *"But I say this to those who are listening: love your enemies! Do good to those who hate you, bless those who curse you, pray for those who treat you badly. To anyone who slaps you on one cheek, present to him the other, to anyone who takes your cloak; do not refuse him your tunic. ...And if you do good to those who do good to you, what credit do you get? For even sinners do the same."*
> (Lk 6:27-29-32)

Jesus, I adore and thank You, because You speak clearly to me. I realize that I always repay evil with evil, that I did not love those who hated me, that I did not bless those who cursed me. My heart is so grudging! I am so prejudiced and so far away from Your love and from the way You want me to love. While I am in Adoration before You, I open my heart and desire to become capable of loving.

(Reflect on and present to Jesus your personal situation and continue to pray for the gift of love.)

224

6) Jesus, I adore You and thank You because You loved the Father without condition. You suffered, You accepted the cross and death, and bitterness never held control in Your heart. I now present to You those who suffer terribly in heart and soul, the sick, the threatened, parents with sick children, those who in suffering, lost their faith and trust in the Father's love and mercy and continue to ask themselves: "Why, O God?" Jesus, send them Your Holy Spirit! May He give them the answers they are looking for, may He comfort them and drive mistrust, fear and bitterness from their hearts so that they are released to love once again.

Heal the love in the hearts of those who help the suffering and aid them in accepting their crosses.

- Jesus, heal love in the hearts of those who are smothered by suffering.

(Repeat this invocation quietly within yourself)

7) Jesus, I adore You and thank You because, in suffering, You loved and this suffering was the birth of our salvation. Bless all those who suffer because they have not converted. By their way of life, they create suffering for themselves, for their families, their friends and their countries. Jesus, I include those who hate, those who do not forgive, those who are full of pride, those who are jealous and envious, those taking alcohol and drugs, those involved in sexual immorality, those who have become criminals. I also pray, Jesus, for those who let themselves be led by a spirit of violence, those who have destroyed the lives of the unborn, those who have taken the lives of others. We suffer because of our sins and then

ask God: "Why?" Enlighten us and enable us to accept Your love, and to convert so that, through Your love, all suffering caused by sin, turns for our good and for Your glory.

- Heal the love in those who are destroying themselves because they have not yet converted! (*Repeat this invocation quietly within yourself and present people you know*)

8) Jesus, I adore You because You are love. You suffered for all of us in love and gave Your life for us. It was not difficult for You to live because You loved. You died, and not even death was hard for You, because You knew that Your sacrifice opened up the way for the salvation of humanity. Jesus, You are life, because You accepted death and ascended into eternal life. With Your death, You gave a meaning to our lives and our deaths, to the sick and the healthy, to the young and the old. Jesus, You give meaning to every life, to every situation, even when everything seems to have been wasted and it is difficult to make sense out of it. Jesus, I present to You all the young who cannot find meaning in their lives, who have not yet learned the secret of sacrificing themselves for others, who have not yet discovered that real happiness lies in helping one another. Grant that they understand that life is a gift and that the most beautiful lesson is to learn to do things for others. Grant that they discover the beauty and the joy in every gesture of love. May peace and love return to their hearts and be their way, their truth and their lives.

- Jesus, heal the love in those who love nothing and no one, and who doubt that life has meaning. (*Repeat this invocation quietly within yourself*)

9) Jesus, I adore You and thank You because You were guided by love to come to deliver us from evil and death and to save us. Listen now to the cries of those who are victims of war, of terror, of violence, of injustice and deception. Grant that all those who feel unloved and rejected may meet Your gaze full of love and compassion. Grant that those who are looking for support, for a friendly hand, for help, may accept Your hand. Purify this world with Your love especially wherever I go, cleanse them from hatred and violence and grant us Your peace. (*Present the world situation to Jesus and decide to change it in some small way, starting with yourself*)

10) Blessing

O Jesus, love the Father, say only the Word and our hearts will be healed and peace and love will return. With Your infinite love, nurse our wounds and enter into the hearts of every one of us, especially in the hearts of those who feel alone and forgotten by all. May Your love reach every heart and invent new ways for overcoming division, rancor and loneliness. Jesus, say only the Word and our love will be healed. You who live an reign world without end. Amen.

THE NEW RHYTHM!

Man is a being who poses questions, who needs answers and looks for meaning in almost everything he does. And so it is with prayer also. Why and for whom do we pray? These are the first questions of all those who believe. The real answer comes only after we have begun to pray, when we have an experience of the fruits of prayer and we know how beautiful it is to spend time with God.

The first fruit of prayer is inner peace which never abandons us, not in times of well-being and no tin times of suffering. This peace is like an interior weighing scales, which controls our psychological, moral, and spiritual balance, and prevents us from collapsing under the strain of suffering or becoming full of pride when all is well. This peace permits us to keep our feet on the ground with our gaze faced towards the heavens. This inner peace creates a new rhythm for our souls, for our hearts and for our whole being.

There are many things and many situations which pull a person out of his normal rhythm, out of his peace. When one loses one's rhythm, one's pace, then one's existential balance is easily lost also, and it is this which brings us down unforeseen streets and wrong roads! Our tension, our anger, our bad language, our abuse of alcohol and drugs, our bickering and fighting, our dissatisfaction, our grumblings, our insecurities, our fears and anguishes, our insomnia are some of the signs which show that we have lost our natural rhythm, that inner peace, that allows us to meet with God, with others and with ourselves.

In order to enter into the natural rhythm, it is essential to find the time and space for prayer. Today, we need to pray even more because the dangers and situations which can knock us out of rhythm are much more numerous. The faithful who pray superficially and in a hurry do not enter into this new rhythm and, therefore, cannot change anything in their lives. For this reason, it is possible to find those addicted to drugs and alcohol even among the faithful.

Only sincere, profound prayer can reach the heart of the Father, and thereby, heal and save us. This consumer atmosphere and materialistic society which we have today creates addicts. Humanity today has ever increasing and ever renewing needs and we feel that, in order to survive, we have to satisfy all our desires and all our needs, and we do not realize that, as we continue, we immerse ourselves ever deeper in unhappiness, apathy and senselessness. Fi humanity does not return to God, to itself, to one another and to nature, then humanity will destroy itself.

Every baby, in its first few months of life, sleeps up to twenty hours a day. If the baby does not sleep it is because somehow it has lost its peace. Peace I the necessary condition for its growth and development. Disturbance and agitation are the beginnings of death.

Dear friend, I wish for your prayer to be profound and true. These prayers will introduce you to a new rhythm in which nothing and no one can take you away from God, from yourselves or from each other. If we continue in prayer, we will always have inner peace and profound joy despite the mishaps in daily life.

Finally, let us listen to the words of the Queen of Peace, and may Her prayer be put into practice in our daily lives:

"Dear children! Today, I rejoice with you and I am praying with you for peace: peace in your hearts, peace in your families, peace in your desires, peace in the whole world. May the King of Peace bless you today and give you peace. I bless you and I carry each one of you in my heart. Thank you for having responded to my call." (December 25, 1994)